READERS THEATRE
FOR CHILDREN

READERS THEATRE
FOR CHILDREN

Scripts and Script Development

MILDRED KNIGHT LAUGHLIN
University of Oklahoma

KATHY HOWARD LATROBE
University of Oklahoma

TEACHER IDEAS PRESS
A Division of
Libraries Unlimited, Inc.
Englewood, Colorado
1990

TEACHER IDEAS PRESS
A Division of
Libraries Unlimited, Inc.
P.O. Box 3988
Englewood, Colorado 80155-3988

Library of Congress Cataloging-in-Publication Data

Laughlin, Mildred.
    Readers theatre for children : scripts and script development /
Mildred Knight Laughlin, Kathy Howard Latrobe.
    xi, 138p. 22x28 cm.
    Includes bibliographical references.
    ISBN 0-87287-753-1
    1. Readers' theater. 2. Children's plays--Presentation, etc.
3. Children's plays. 4. Stage adaptations. I. Latrobe, Kathy
Howard. II. Title. III. Title: Scripts and script development.
PN2081.R4L39 1990
808.5'45--dc20
                                    90-10713
                                        CIP

For our daughters

Mildred's Barbara and Debra
and
Kathy's Maria and Kimberly

CONTENTS

PART IV—SUGGESTED SCRIPTS

PREFACE

Student enjoyment of literature is a prime concern of all elementary teachers and school librarians, and readers theatre is one technique to use in developing that pleasure. As children interpret prepared scripts representing selections from classic and contemporary works, they help create in an audience the desire to read the works from which the selections were taken.

Children, as they learn the techniques of developing scripts from books they read, are provided with a pleasurable alternative to the traditional book report. The higher levels of thinking skills required to create and share readers theatre effectively make the process in any context a valuable learning experience.

Because there are many approaches used in readers theatre, Part I of this book is designed to provide an overview of the techniques that are recommended and applied by the authors. The importance of readers theatre is emphasized, and directions are given for script selection, scripting techniques, the selection and preparation of readers, and presentation techniques. This introductory section is designed to familiarize teachers with the readers theatre process and to guide them in teaching children to use the technique.

Following Part I, scripts and suggested scripts are presented in Parts II, III, and IV. Part II includes twelve completed scripts from selected classics. Part III gives an introduction to a readers theatre program featuring ten novels by Betsy Byars and includes suggestions for creating scripts for each of the books. Part IV provides forty-five suggested scripts selected from children's books that have literary excellence, reader appeal, and the potential for easily created readers theatre scripts.

Part I
READERS THEATRE

INTRODUCTION

WHAT READERS THEATRE IS

Readers theatre is a presentation by two or more participants who read from scripts and interpret a literary work in such a way that the audience imaginatively senses characterization, setting, and action. Voice and body tension rather than movement are involved, thus eliminating the need for the many practice sessions that timing and action techniques require in the presentation of a play. Because children sit and read the lines, they can concentrate on voice interpretation, an essential aspect of communication skill development. Since the audience participates imaginatively, no costuming, make-up, scenery, or stage movement is required. Occasionally, an entrance or exit by one of the readers aids in character interpretation and is therefore appropriate. If a scarf or hat or a certain color of clothes will allow the audience more easily to identify the reader as a given character, such a costume suggestion is appropriate but not essential.

Techniques for readers theatre presentations vary. In this work suggestions will focus on effective voice interpretation that will allow the audience to sense the emotions involved. The reader's focus of attention while speaking will be on the audience rather than on other participants. The "onstage" focus utilized when presenting a play becomes a distraction in readers theatre. It is important, however, that the participants focus their attention on the person reading unless the script demands otherwise.

In addition, this book emphasizes techniques through which children will learn to adapt a scene from a favorite book to make it appropriate for readers theatre. Original script-writing will not be covered, because an important purpose of this book is to urge utilization of a medium through which good literature will be enjoyed. Young people who enjoy reading can often inspire their peers to read a particular book when it is introduced through readers theatre.

VALUE OF READERS THEATRE

Because children usually enjoy theatre-type presentations, readers theatre is fun. This pleasurable introduction to a book with literary quality will often make the audience look forward to reading the entire work. In general, readers theatre is far superior to book reports as a way for young people to share books they have read.

In order for children to prepare an effective script, they often will need to read a number of books to find a scene they wish to adapt. To apply the criteria for appropriate scene selection, the children unconsciously become critical readers. In addition, their knowledge of quality literature is extended.

Communication skills are enhanced as children become cognizant of voice projection, appropriate inflection, and accurate pronunciation of words. Children become familar with new words and extend their vocabulary. Effective scripts often employ language with rich imagery to help the audience better imagine the scene.

Many children fear the experience of standing alone in front of their peers and sharing information. The opportunity to read while seated in a shared presentation, without the audience's attention being constantly focused on one person, helps develop confidence and poise.

Many teachers and librarians plan practice activities involving an entire class in experiences that stretch the imagination and make students sensitive to emotions portrayed by voice. These guided sharing sessions can also help young people become sensitive to the needs of others and respect their efforts. Then, as children plan and work together on a specific readers theatre script, they have opportunities to evidence respect for the opinions of others and recognize the value of cooperative activity.

Participation in readers theatre demands creative thinking. The audience must suspend disbelief, view the reader as a character in a book rather than as a classmate, and become involved in the mood of the scene. As readers and audience evaluate the success of the performance, they must also apply critical thinking skills.

Scripting affords many opportunities to develop writing skills. After an appropriate scene is selected, the child preparing the script must decide what information can best be presented by a narrator. Lines may need to be omitted or adapted in order for the audience to understand the scene. An introduction must always be written to introduce the characters and set the scene. Then, the narrator usually needs to close the scene with a final punch line that will inspire the audience to read the entire work.

As part of the audience, children must employ concentrated listening if they are going to understand fully the scene being presented. As they hear the scene, the audience must imaginatively create setting, character, and mood. This involvement often means that the listener understands the scene better than if he or she were reading it silently. Helping children develop imagination skills is especially important because children today are accustomed to the visuals of television to enhance the understanding of lines spoken. Readers theatre demands creative listeners.

HOW TO SELECT AND PREPARE READERS

In selecting readers for readers theatre in the classroom or library, it is important to remember that the purpose of the activity is to introduce literature and that the activity is designed to be a learning experience rather than a polished performance. Enthusiasm and the desire to interpret the script in the most effective manner are essential characteristics of effective participants.

It is important when possible that the readers have read the entire work from which the selection is taken. This allows them to understand the emotions of the character and that person's involvement in the story conflict. If the appropriate number of readers has volunteered to participate, it may be well to ask each volunteer to read the entire script before the characters are assigned. Sometimes the teacher or librarian may wish to read the script aloud as each young person reads silently. This procedure helps to avoid problems in the pronunciation of words and gives the readers a sense of the emotional impact of the selection. However, the librarian or teacher must be aware of a negative aspect of this approach. Some readers may attempt to imitate the teacher or librarian instead of using their own imagination and creativity in presenting the lines.

A better approach may be for the group to discuss the plot of the entire work and place the scene to be read in perspective. Then the group can read the entire script aloud, taking turns so that all have the opportunity to read. A discussion of each character's personality and of the mood to be evoked in the scene should follow the first reading.

At this time, the pronunciation of difficult words can be clarified. Also, participants can discuss the interpretative directions that are inserted in the script. It may be well for two or three readers to try to interpret the lines angrily, hesitantly, etc., as the notes in parentheses indicate. This is particularly helpful to novice readers. In addition, it may be helpful for the entire group to discuss why the author used certain verbs or adjectives. Such a discussion may heighten each reader's sensitivity to the script, to the role of each character, and to the emotional involvement desired for the audience.

Readers may volunteer for roles or roles may be assigned by group consensus. After each reader highlights his or her speeches with a pencil or felt-tipped pen and reads those lines silently, the whole script may be read again with each participant reading the appropriate segments. Then, the group may want to set a time for additional group reading before the scene is presented to an audience.

Because it can be assumed that all members of a class will want to be involved in a readers theatre presentation at some time, the whole class should participate in activities involving voice projection, emotional responses, and interpretive body movements. The suggested activities that follow are only a few that may be used to practice skills that are appropriate not only for readers theatre but also for communication in general. For a voice projection exercise, the teacher or librarian first may want to whisper instructions in a voice so soft that the majority of the group cannot hear. As the young people express their annoyance, the adult may respond by shouting the directions in a voice far too loud for easy listening. This can prompt a discussion of effective voice projection.

A good practice activity for follow-up is to have pairs of students stand opposite each other about a yard apart, introduce themselves, and then tell the other person what their favorite food is. At nine feet apart the pair should repeat the introduction, this time identifying a favorite sport. At about eighteen feet apart they talk about a favorite book. This exercise should take place in an auditorium or multipurpose room if possible so that the distance apart can continue to be increased. The students should be practicing the ideas discussed earlier and not shouting. At the end of the exercise, they might hold a short rap session to discuss the techniques they used to project their voice effectively.

Tongue twisters are effective for emphasizing correct, clear pronunciations. It is also a good idea to have children pronounce words that are often mispronounced or slurred, such as "getting" and "just."

There are many activities that can be used that demand an emotional response. A group exercise in contrasts can be initiated by asking someone to respond to the question, "Would you like to go out to eat?" by saying in a *bored* tone, "No, unless there's nothing here that I like." After two or three of the group have responded, others can practice an *enthusiastic* response to the same question: "Yes, can we go to McDonald's?"

"Will you pick up these papers?" can elicit a *rude* response, "No, I wasn't the one who threw them there," or a *polite* response, "Yes, I'm sorry I didn't notice them scattered around." Similar questions can show the contrast of *nervously* and *confidently, brave* and *fearfully,* and so forth. Students may want to make up their own examples and share with the group.

It is often necessary for a reader to make a bodily response to someone else's lines or to pretend a simple action. Practicing basic pantomime activities that do not require getting up from a seated position is helpful in building awareness of the communication power of body movements. Suggest that members of the class volunteer to do simple activities such as pretending to read a book, answering the imaginary telephone that is ringing, trembling in fear, wiping the forehead in frustration, and handing someone an imaginary object. Discuss what caused the pantomime to be convincing.

PRESENTATION TECHNIQUES

Because the setting is imagined by the audience, seating is an important consideration. The arrangement of the characters on the stage can be the means by which the audience sees character relationships. Readers may be seated on the floor, on stools, or on chairs. For some scripts, positioning a leading character in the center on a stool will indicate importance.

If two different groups interact, one early and another late in the scene, the more involved character may be in the center, and the grouping on each side can show event progression. Experiment with seating until the desired relationship is achieved. Although in most instances the entire cast of readers is seated when the scene begins, there are rare occasions when a late arrival or an early exit is necessary to enhance the audience's understanding of the scene or to help create an appropriate mood.

Usually a straight line of readers is avoided unless dictated by the script, as would be the case if the setting were the back seat of a bus. All characters should be placed to face the audience so the facial expression of each can be seen. The narrator usually stands at one side, facing the audience and using a lectern for the script. As the characters are introduced by the narrator, each should nod as his or her name is called so that the audience can begin to recognize the role of each.

If the readers so wish, they may wear clothing colors that reflect the mood of the scene. Dark colors may be chosen for serious presentations and lighter colors for humorous scenes. Readers should wear clothing that does not distract the audience. Noisy jewelry should be avoided. An accessory appropriate to a character may be used, such as a baseball cap or a bright scarf, to assist the audience in quick character identification.

The size and style of the script should be uniform. A black construction paper cover is often used. Scripts typed in pamphlet style with a center fold are easier to manage. All readers should not turn the page at the same time, as this action can be distracting to the audience. Readers should be so familiar with the dialogue that they can follow the lines and at the same time maintain eye contact with the audience during reading.

Because the audience is actively and imaginatively involved in the text, the focus of the readers should be on the audience rather than on one another. Characters do not look directly at their fellow readers as they deliver their lines; instead, they focus at a point somewhere in the audience. This offstage focus keeps the concentration of the audience on the lines rather than on the readers.

Voice projection is essential in readers theatre. If the reader is constantly alert to the lines, both mentally and physically, and is concentrating on the scene, it is easier to read with expression and be heard by the audience. The reader must imagine that he or she is experiencing the emotions evident in the lines. The reader must create word pictures for the audience. All readers should listen to the speeches of others and be aware of the mood. Even though the scene has been practiced, the presentation should be enthusiastic and have a first-time feel.

HOW TO SELECT A LITERARY WORK TO ADAPT

Although fiction with plenty of dialogue provides the most popular and easily adapted sources for readers theatre scripts, other genres of literature also offer rich possibilities. Biography, folklore, and poetry may also be used. For example, Paul Fleischman's Newbery-award poetry *Joyful Noise* (Harper, 1988) provides creative two-part presentations for reading. Because it offers readers the opportunity to speak different lines simultaneously, an unusual effect results. A series of these poems with narrator introduction and tie-ins (easy to write because of the insect theme) can constitute a creative, thought-provoking presentation.

Although plays may be a source of scripts, in general they are more difficult for the novice scriptwriter to select and adapt. In plays, the dependence upon action to assist the audience in understanding the lines is a stumbling block for meaningful adaptation to readers theatre format.

Scripts for readers theatre can be adapted from a wide range of materials; but if the purpose is to introduce children to quality literature, then literary excellence is an important consideration. In addition, the selection should have dramatic appeal so that the excerpt used will evoke the desired audience reaction and interaction. The dramatic conflict in which the characters engage need not demand physical action. The conflict can be within the character, with the action suggested through narration and conversation. Though some action may be summarized by the narrator, the audience is more involved when the implied action is part of the dialogue. If the listeners are to enjoy and remember the experience, the selection must be a meaningful whole that gives an insight into the entire book.

The selection chosen must have emotional appeal, stimulating the imagination of the listeners and deepening their response. This involvement necessitates unique characters who strongly interact to arouse audience interest.

It is much simpler to adapt a script if the scene selected is dominated by conversation and includes a limited number of characters. Audience interest and emotional involvement is deterred if the narrator dominates the scene. If there are too many characters, the audience has difficulty in identifying each speaker and in establishing the necessary relationships among characters.

To increase audience enjoyment the language used in the dialogue should be provocative. Through the use of sensory images, thought-provoking references, and figurative language, the listener is able to relate imaginatively to each character.

SCRIPTING TECHNIQUES

Scripting techniques vary according to the nature of the literary work being adapted, the experience of the person developing the script, the experiences the readers and audience bring to readers theatre, and time constraints. The following suggestions for preparing scripts are general in nature and have been developed as guidelines for teachers and librarians as they assist children in adapting a literary segment for presentation.

1. Read the entire work from which a selection is to be adapted. Consider the author's purpose for writing the book, the theme, and the scene or scenes that will best reflect the whole. After the portion of the work to be presented is chosen, read that portion again to mark those lines that must be kept if the selection is to be understood by the audience. If a copier is available, it may be advantageous to reproduce those pages and use a felt-tipped pen to highlight necessary dialogue.

2. Reread the selection and omit unnecessary description or narration. If needed, insert narrator lines to bridge gaps, show lapses of time, or summarize action. In general, authors identify speakers to the reader through a "she said" type of approach. However, in reader theatre it is often necessary to include the name of the person to whom the conversation is directed to assist the audience in quick character identification.

3. Too many readers on stage are confusing to the audience, so it is appropriate, if needed, to eliminate minor characters and give their lines to major characters. This combining of characters' lines must be done without destroying the spirit of the scene, however. Some specialists in readers theatre advise using one reader for two characters. If this approach must be taken, a slight costume modification (for example, the addition of a hat or glasses) may be the means by which the audience can quickly identify the speaker. If possible, avoid the need for duplication of roles.

4. As appropriate, add to the script a description of the tone of voice—e.g., "shyly" and any needed gesture or facial expression that might assist the reader in interpreting the lines. The person preparing the script has a greater understanding of the whole work and a better feeling for the desired

emotional impact than any one reader has, even though all presenters should have read the entire book.

5. Type the final version of the script. Double spacing assists the reader, and bold-face capital letters giving each character's name should precede the lines of dialogue. Specific directions for tone of voice or gesture should follow the character's name and be indicated in parentheses so that the reader will not be confused. These directions may also be included within the speech if a change of tone or slight body action is needed. When the script demands a nonverbal communication of emotion by a person who is not reading, that character should be identified in the script in bold type as though he or she were speaking, and appropriate directions should be given in parentheses.

Prepare scripts on legal-size paper turned to the side to create two columns of type. Staple the sheets in the center to resemble a pamphlet and cover with black paper so that the script will appear unobtrusive to the audience. At the beginning of the script identify the type and location of the seating for each character.

6. In addition to identifying the characters' names, the narrator, in his or her opening speech, might give very brief descriptions to help the audience remember who the characters are. The narrator should also give any needed information about preceding events and identify the setting so that the audience will understand the scene to be presented. In the few instances in which a story is told in the first person and a narrator is unnecessary, the character telling the story usually introduces the characters and scene.

Although the portion of the literary work presented is a complete, meaningful segment, the narrator usually closes the presentation with summary lines tying the scene to the entire work, indicating theme and conflict, as appropriate, and suggesting the types of events that are to come. But care must be taken not to reveal too much of the plot; doing so would perhaps spoil the enjoyment of members of the audience who may wish to read the book.

If more than one scene is presented consecutively, the narrator usually provides a link between the scenes. Characters may change positions between scenes as the script dictates.

EVALUATION

The positive reaction of the audience to the presentation is the best evidence of its success. Increased reading by young people of the book from which the selection was taken should be another indicator of the value of the presentation. As readers theatre becomes a part of classroom or library activities, improved audience listening skills, increased desire by young people to write their own scripts, and more sensitive reading of lines should result.

As part of the development of effective communication skills, some teachers or librarians may want the audience and readers to discuss the presentation. If so, it is wise to begin with all the positive, exciting things. As suggestions for improvement are made, the character's name rather than the reader's name should be used. This approach directs the discussion to character interpretation rather than to reader criticism. Above all, nothing should deter students from enjoying readers theatre as a pleasurable activity, just as reading should be pleasurable.

Part II
COMPLETED SCRIPTS

LITTLE WOMEN

Louisa May Alcott

This script is taken from chapter 1 as the four sisters make plans for Christmas.

STAGING:
The narrator stands at a lectern. Meg and Amy sit on chairs. Beth and Jo are seated on the floor.

Meg   Amy
X   X

Beth   Jo
X   X

Narrator
X

NARRATOR: We shall share the first scene in *Little Women* by Louisa May Alcott. The characters are pretty, brown-haired, sixteen-year-old Meg, read by _____; tall, thin, fifteen-year-old Jo, a bookworm who cares little about how she looks, read by _____; shy, trusting, thirteen-year-old Beth, read by _____; and slender, blue-eyed, mannerly Amy, the youngest, but most important, to her way of thinking, read by _____. I, _____, am the narrator.

    As the scene opens, it is evening and the four sisters are sitting in front of the fireplace waiting for their mother to come home. They are discussing Christmas plans.

JO: (grumbling) Christmas won't be Christmas without any presents.

MEG: (sighing) It's so dreadful to be poor!

AMY: (sniffing) I don't think it's fair for some girls to have plenty of pretty things, and other girls nothing at all.

BETH: (cheerfully) We've got father and mother and each other.

JO: (sadly) We haven't got father. You know he's far away where the fighting is, and we shall not have him for a long time.

MEG: You know the reason Mother proposed not having any presents this Christmas was because it is going to be a hard winter for everyone. She thinks we ought not to spend money for pleasure when our men are suffering so in the army. We can't do much, but we can make our little sacrifices, and we ought to do it gladly. But I am afraid I can't (shaking her head regretfully).

JO: Meg, I don't think the little we would spend would do them any good. We've each got a dollar, and the army wouldn't be much helped by our giving that. I agree not to expect anything from mother or you, but I do want to buy a book for myself that I have wanted for *so* long.

BETH: I planned to spend mine on new music.

AMY: (decidedly) I intend to get a nice box of drawing pencils. I really need them.

JO: Mother didn't say anything about our money, and she won't wish us to give up everything. Let's each buy what we want, and have a little fun. I'm sure we work hard enough to earn it.

MEG: (complaining) I know *I* do, Jo. I teach those tiresome children nearly all day, when I'm longing to enjoy myself at home.

JO: Meg, you don't have half such a hard time as I do. How would you like to be shut up for hours with a nervous, fussy old lady? She keeps you trotting, is never satisfied, and worries you till you're ready to fly out the window or cry.

BETH: (sighing as she looks at her hands) It's naughty to fret; but I do think washing dishes and keeping things tidy is the worst work in the world. It makes me cross; and my hands get so stiff, I can't practice well at all.

AMY: Beth, I don't think any of you suffer as I do. You don't have to go to school with impertinent girls, who plague you if you don't know your lessons. They laugh at your dresses, and label your father if he isn't rich, and insult you when your nose isn't nice.

JO: (laughing) If you mean *libel,* Amy, I'd say so, and not talk about *labels* as if papa were a pickle bottle.

AMY: (with dignity) I know what I mean, Jo, and you needn't be *satirical* about it. It's proper to use good words and improve your *vocabulary.*

MEG: (seriously) Don't peck at one another. Don't you wish we had the money papa lost when we were little, Jo? Dear me! How happy and good we'd be, if we had no worries!

BETH: Meg, you said the other day you thought we were a great deal happier than the King children, who fight and fret all the time in spite of their money.

MEG: So I did, Beth. Well, I think we are; for though we do have to work, we make fun for ourselves, and are a pretty jolly set, as Jo would say.

AMY: (reproving) Jo does use such slang words!

JO: (begins to whistle)

AMY: Don't whistle, Jo, it's so boyish.

JO: That's why I do it.

AMY: I detest rude, unladylike girls!

JO: I hate affected niminy, piminy brats.

BETH: (smiling) Birds in their little nests must agree.

MEG: (lecturing) Really, girls, you are both to be blamed. You are old enough to leave off boyish tricks and to behave better, Josephine. It didn't matter so much when you were a little girl, but now you are so tall and turn up your hair. You should remember that you are a young lady.

JO: (shaking her head) I'm not! If turning up my hair makes me one, I'll wear it in two tails till I'm twenty. I hate to think I've got to grow up and be Miss March, and wear long gowns and look as prim as a China aster! It's bad enough to be a girl, anyway, when I like boys' games and work and manners! I can't get over my disappointment in not being a boy, and it's worse than ever now. I'm dying to go and fight with papa, and I can only stay home and knit like a poky old woman!

BETH: Poor Jo! It's too bad, but it can't be helped. You must try to be contented with making your name boyish, and playing brother to us girls.

MEG: As for you, Amy, you are altogether too particular and prim. Your airs are funny now; but you'll grow up to be an affected little goose if you don't take care. I like your nice manners and refined way of speaking when you don't try to be elegant, but your absurd words are as bad as Jo's slang.

BETH: If Jo is a tomboy and Amy is a goose, Meg, what am I, please?

MEG:	(lovingly) You're a dear, Beth, and nothing else.
JO:	It's six o'clock. Mother will be here any minute. I must warm her slippers as she'll be tired. Oh, dear, Mother's house slippers are quite worn out. She must have a new pair.
BETH:	I thought I'd get her some with my dollar.
AMY:	(quickly) No, Beth, I shall!
MEG:	(firmly) I'm the oldest.
JO:	(interrupting) I'm the man of the family now that papa is away. I shall provide the slippers, for he told me to take special care of Mother while he was gone.
BETH:	I'll tell you what we'll do. Let's each get *her* something for Christmas, and not get anything for ourselves.
JO:	(excitedly) That's like you, Beth. What will we get!
MEG:	(looking at her hands) I shall give her a nice pair of gloves.
JO:	Walking shoes, best to be had!
BETH:	Some handkerchiefs, all hemmed.
AMY:	I'll get a little bottle of cologne. She likes it, and it won't cost much, so I'll have some money left to buy my pencils.
MEG:	How will we give the things?
JO:	We'll put them on the table, and bring her in and see her open the bundles. Don't you remember how we used to do on our birthdays? We'll let Mother think we're getting things for ourselves and then surprise her. We must go shopping tomorrow afternoon, Meg.
NARRATOR:	Christmas proves to be special, and at a New Year's Eve dance, Jo meets Laurie, who lives next door with his grandfather. Jo and Laurie become special friends, and they increasingly depend on each other in the days that follow—days filled with both happiness and heartaches.

SCRIPTING NOTES:

1. Much of the conversation in the book involves long sentences. These have often been divided for easier reading.

2. The names of the characters have often been inserted into the conversation so that the audience can become familiar with the four sisters.

3. The word "Mother" was substituted for the girls' pet name "Marmie."

4. Unnecessary movement has been omitted.

THE WONDERFUL WIZARD OF OZ

L. Frank Baum

This script is taken from an early chapter in which Dorothy meets the Scarecrow.

STAGING:

The narrator stands at a lectern. Dorothy and Scarecrow sit on stools.

Dorothy   Scarecrow

X   X

Narrator

X

NARRATOR: The script that we are reading is taken from *The Wonderful Wizard of Oz,* by L. Frank Baum. The characters are Dorothy, a young girl who was blown by a Kansas cyclone to the Land of Oz, read by _____, and the brainless Scarecrow, read by _____. I, _____, am the narrator.

Dorothy wants to leave the Land of Oz and go back to Kansas. The good Witch of the North tells her to follow the yellow brick road to the City of Emeralds where Oz may help her. As she walks along with her dog, Toto, she sees a scarecrow placed high on a pole.

SCARECROW: Good-day.

DOROTHY: (surprised) Did you speak?

SCARECROW: Certainly. How do you do?

DOROTHY: (politely) I'm pretty well, thank you. How do *you* do?

SCARECROW: I'm not feeling well. It is very tedious being perched up here night and day to scare away crows.

DOROTHY: Can't you get down?

SCARECROW: No, for this pole is stuck up my back. If you will please take away the pole, I shall be greatly obliged to you.

DOROTHY: That won't be hard. You are stuffed with straw and are quite light. I'll set you here on the ground.

SCARECROW:	Thank you very much. I feel like a new man. Who are you and where are you going?
DOROTHY:	My name is Dorothy, and I am going to the Emerald City to ask the great Oz to send me back to Kansas.
SCARECROW:	Where is the Emerald City, and who is Oz?
DOROTHY:	(surprised) Don't you know?
SCARECROW:	(sadly) No, indeed I don't know anything. You see, I am stuffed, so I have no brains at all.
DOROTHY:	Oh, I'm awfully sorry for you.
SCARECROW:	Do you think that if I go to the Emerald City with you, that Oz would give me some brains?
DOROTHY:	I cannot tell, but you may come with me if you like. If Oz will not give you any brains you will be no worse off than you are now.
SCARECROW:	That is true. You see, I don't mind my legs and arms and body being stuffed because I cannot get hurt. If anyone treads on me or sticks a pin into me, it doesn't matter for I can't feel it. But I do not want people to call me a fool. If my head stays stuffed with straw instead of with brains, as yours is, how am I ever to know everything?
DOROTHY:	I understand how you feel. I am truly sorry for you. If you will come with me, I'll ask Oz to do all he can for you.
SCARECROW:	Thank you. Let's go.
DOROTHY:	Don't mind Toto. He growls but he never bites.
SCARECROW:	Oh, I'm not afraid. He can't hurt the straw. Do let me carry that basket for you. I shall not mind it, for I can't get tired. I'll tell you a secret. There is only one thing in the world I am afraid of.
DOROTHY:	What is that? Is it the Munchkin farmer who made you?
SCARECROW:	No, I'm afraid of a lighted match.
NARRATOR:	At noon they sit down by the roadside near a little brook. Dorothy opens her basket and gets out some bread.
DOROTHY:	Would you like a piece of bread?
SCARECROW:	No, thank you, I am never hungry. It is a lucky thing I am not. My mouth

is only painted, and if I should cut a hole in it so I can eat, the straw I am stuffed with would fall out. That would spoil the shape of my head.

DOROTHY: (nodding) I see.

SCARECROW: Tell me something about yourself, and the country you came from.

DOROTHY: I lived on a farm in Kansas with my Aunt Em and Uncle Henry. When you stood in the doorway and looked around, you could see nothing but the great gray prairie on every side. Uncle Henry and Aunt Em never laughed. They worked hard from morning till night and never knew what joy was. Then one day a cyclone came. Aunt Em climbed down the ladder into the cellar and told me to follow. Before I could catch Toto, the cyclone lifted the house into the air like a balloon. When it set down, I was in Oz.

SCARECROW: I can't understand why you should wish to leave this beautiful country and go back to the dry gray place you call Kansas.

DOROTHY: That is because you have no brains. No matter how dreary and gray our homes are, we people of flesh and blood would rather live there than in any other country, be it ever so beautiful. There is no place like home.

SCARECROW: Of course I can't understand it. If your heads were stuffed with straw, like mine, you would probably all live in the beautiful places, and then Kansas would have no people at all. It is fortunate for Kansas that you have brains.

DOROTHY: Won't you tell *me* a story while we are resting?

SCARECROW: My life has been so short that I really know nothing whatever. I was made only day before yesterday. What happened in the world before that is unknown to me. But I wasn't a good scarecrow. An old crow just sat on my shoulder and said any crow of sense could see I was only stuffed with straw. Then he and a great flock ate all the corn they wanted. I felt sad at this but the old crow told me that if I only had brains in my head, I would be as good a man as any of them. The old crow said that brains are the only things worth having in the world. By good luck, you came along, and from what you say I am sure the great Oz will give me brains as soon as we get to the Emerald City.

DOROTHY: (earnestly) I hope so since you seem anxious to have them.

SCARECROW: Oh, yes, I *am* anxious. It is such an uncomfortable feeling to know one is a fool.

DOROTHY: Well, let us take this road into the forest.

SCARECROW: If this road goes in, it must come out. As the Emerald City is at the other end of the road, we must go wherever it leads us.

DOROTHY: Anyone would know that.

SCARECROW: Certainly, that is why I know it. If it required brains to figure it out, I never should have said it.

NARRATOR: As Dorothy and the Scarecrow walk on, they meet other troubled friends who need The Wizard's help. They have many exciting adventures before Dorothy finds herself sitting again on the broad Kansas prairie.

SCRIPTING NOTES:

1. Description was used to write Dorothy's speech to Scarecrow about Kansas.

2. The Scarecrow's story was much longer in the text and was summarized to avoid slowing the pace.

THE SECRET GARDEN

Frances Hodgson Burnett

This script is taken from the chapter, "I Am Colin," in which Mary discovers Colin late one night.

STAGING:
The narrator stands at a lectern. Mary and Colin sit on stools.

Mary   Colin

X   X

Narrator

X

NARRATOR: We are sharing a scene from *The Secret Garden* by Frances Hodgson Burnett. The characters in this scene are two spoiled and lonely cousins who at the turn of the century live in Misselthwaite Manor, an isolated mansion in Yorkshire, England. Mary, read by _____, is an orphan who has been sent to Misselthwaite to be in her uncle's care. Colin, read by _____, is the uncle's sickly boy who refuses to have guests or to leave his room. Neither knows the other lives at Misselthwaite. I, _____, am the narrator.

     Late at night Mary has been listening to the rain and the wind beating against the windows, and she has heard mysterious and mournful crying. It is not the first time Mary has heard the crying, but this time she decides that she will find out what it is. After wandering down long, shadowy hallways, she opens a door, and there inside is Colin crying fretfully. Each is surprised.

COLIN: (in a loud whisper) Who are you? Are you a ghost?

MARY: (in a loud whisper) No, I am not. Are you one?

COLIN: No. I am Colin.

MARY: (hesitating) Who is Colin?

COLIN: I am Colin Craven. Who are you?

MARY: I am Mary Lennox. Mr. Craven is my uncle.

COLIN: He is my father.

MARY: (gasping) Your father! No one ever told me he had a boy! Why didn't they?

COLIN: You are real, aren't you? I have such real dreams very often. You might be one of them. Where did you come from?

MARY: From my own room. The wind wuthered and moaned so I couldn't go to sleep, and I heard someone crying and wanted to find out who it was. What were you crying for?

COLIN: Because I couldn't go to sleep either and my head ached. Tell me your name again.

MARY: Mary Lennox. Did no one ever tell you I had come to live here?

COLIN: No. They daren't.

MARY: Why?

COLIN: Because I should have been afraid you would see me. I won't let people see and talk me over.

MARY: Why?

COLIN: Because I am like this always, ill and having to lie down. My father won't let people talk me over either. The servants are not allowed to speak about me. If I live I may be a hunchback, but I shan't live. My father hates to think I may be like him.

MARY: Oh, what a strange house this is! What a strange house! Everything is a kind of secret. Rooms are locked up and gardens are locked up—and you! Have you been locked up?

COLIN: No. I stay in this room because I don't want to be moved out of it. It tires me too much.

MARY: Does your father come and see you?

COLIN: Sometimes. Generally when I am asleep. He doesn't want to see me.

MARY: Why?

COLIN: (slightly angry) My mother died when I was born, and it makes him wretched to look at me. He thinks I don't know, but I've heard people talking. He almost hates me.

MARY: (half speaking to herself) He hates the garden because she died.

COLIN: What garden?

NARRATOR: At this point Mary hesitates because she does not want to tell Colin that she has found both the secret garden and its key.

MARY: (slowly) Oh! just—just a garden she used to like. Have you been here always?

COLIN: Nearly always. Sometimes I have been taken to places at the seaside, but I won't stay because people stare at me. I used to wear an iron thing to keep my back straight, but a grand doctor came from London to see me and said it was stupid. He told them to take it off and keep me out in the fresh air. I hate fresh air and I don't want to go out.

MARY: I didn't when first I came here. Why do you keep looking at me like that?

COLIN: Because of the dreams that are so real. Sometimes when I open my eyes I don't believe I'm awake.

MARY: We're both awake. It looks quite like a dream, and it's the middle of the night, and everybody in the house is asleep—everybody but us. We are wide awake.

COLIN: (restlessly) I don't want it to be a dream.

MARY: (thinking the thought all at once) If you don't like people to see you, do you want me to go away?

COLIN: No. I should be sure you were a dream if you went. If you are real, talk. I want to hear about you.

MARY: What do you want me to tell you?

NARRATOR: He asks her how long she has been at Misselthwaite; which corridor her room is on; what she has been doing; if she dislikes the moor as he dislikes it; and where she has lived before coming to Yorkshire. She answers all these questions and many more, and he lies back on his pillow and listens. He makes her tell him a great deal about India and about her voyage across the ocean. She finds out that because he has been an invalid he has not learned things as other children have. One of his nurses taught him to read when he was quite little, and he is always reading and looking at pictures in splendid books.

 Though his father rarely sees him when he is awake, he is given all sorts of wonderful things to amuse himself with. He never seems to be amused, however. He can have anything he asks for and is never made to do anything he does not like to do.

COLIN: Everyone is obliged to do what pleases me. It makes me ill to be angry. (matter-of-factly) No one believes I shall live to grow up. (pausing) How old are you?

MARY: I am ten, and so are you.

COLIN: (surprised) How do you know that?

MARY: Because when you were born the garden door was locked and the key was buried. And it has been locked for ten years.

COLIN: (suddenly very interested) What garden door was locked? Who did it? Where was the key buried?

MARY: (nervously) It—it was the garden Mr. Craven hates. He locked the door. No one—no one knew where he buried the key.

COLIN: (persisting eagerly) What sort of garden is it?

MARY: (carefully trying to keep her discovery a secret) No one has been allowed to go into it for ten years.

NARRATOR: Mary realizes too late—the secret is out. Colin is much like Mary. He has nothing to think about and the idea of a hidden garden attracts him as it attracted her. He asks question after question. Where is it? Has she never looked for the door? Has she never asked the gardeners?

MARY: They won't talk about it. I think they have been told not to answer questions.

COLIN: I would make them.

MARY: (frightened) Could you?

COLIN: Everyone is obliged to please me. I told you that. If I were to live, this place would someday belong to me. They all know that. I would make them tell me. Do you want to see the secret garden?

MARY: (in a quiet, low voice) Yes.

COLIN: I do. I don't think I ever really wanted to see anything before, but I want to see that garden. I want the key dug up. I want the door unlocked. I would let them take me there in my chair. That would be getting fresh air. I am going to make them open the door. (excitedly) They have to please me. I will make them take me there, and I will let you go, too.

MARY: (crying out) Oh, don't—don't—don't—don't do that!

COLIN: (amazed) Why? You said you wanted to see it.

MARY: (almost sobbing) I do, but if you make them open the door and take you in like that it will never be a secret again.

COLIN: A secret? What do you mean? Tell me.

MARY: (her words tumbling over one another) You see—you see, if no one knows but ourselves—if there was a door, hidden somewhere under the ivy, and if we could find it, and if we could slip through it together and shut it behind us, and if no one knew anyone was inside, we could call it our garden. We could pretend that—that we were missel thrushes and it was our nest. If we played there almost every day and dug and planted seeds and made it all come alive—don't you see? If the garden was a secret and we could get into it, we could watch the things grow bigger every day, and see how many roses are alive. Oh, don't you see how much nicer it would be if it was a secret?

COLIN: (thoughtfully) I never had a secret, except that one about not living to grow up. They don't know I know that so it is a sort of secret. But I like this kind better.

MARY: (pleading) If you won't make them take you to the garden, perhaps—I feel almost sure I can find out how to get in sometime. And then—if the doctor wants you to go out in your chair, and if you can always do what you want to do, perhaps—perhaps we might find some boy who would push you, and we could go alone and it would always be a secret garden.

COLIN: (slowly) I should—like—that. I should like that. I should not mind fresh air in a secret garden. I think you shall be a secret, too. I will not tell them until they find out.

MARY: I have been here a long time. I shall go away now.

NARRATOR: Mary gets up softly, takes her candle and creeps away without making a sound. Mary has not told Colin that she has found the key and that she has plans to bring the garden to life; those secrets will be revealed later when Colin can be taken to the garden. The quiet secrets of those two will eventually have a great influence on the secret garden, the health of Colin, and all of Misselthwaite.

SCRIPTING NOTES:

1. The scene has been shortened through the elimination of references to movement.

2. Dialogue that does not directly reveal the natures of the characters or that does not focus on the secret garden has been omitted.

3. Punctuation and sentence structure have been edited to facilitate reading.

4. To suggest the meaning of Mary's explanation that the wind wuthered, the words "and moaned" were added.

ALICE'S ADVENTURES IN WONDERLAND

Lewis Carroll

This script is adapted from chapter 7, "A Mad Tea-Party," where Alice meets the March Hare, the Hatter, and the Dormouse.

STAGING:

The narrator stands at a lectern. Alice, the March Hare, the Dormouse, and the Hatter sit in chairs at a table.

March Hare   Dormouse   Hatter

X   X   X

Alice

X

Narrator

X

NARRATOR: The script we are reading has been adapted from *Alice's Adventures in Wonderland* by Lewis Carroll. In this adventure of the mad tea-party, Alice, read by _____, visits the March Hare, read by _____, the Dormouse, read by _____, and the Hatter, read by _____. I, _____, am the narrator.

As this scene begins, Alice sits down with the other three characters who are at a large table set out under a tree. The Dormouse is asleep, and the March Hare and the Hatter, who are having tea, are using the creature for a cushion.

MARCH HARE and HATTER: (crying out together at Alice) No room! No room!

ALICE: (indignantly) There's *plenty* of room!

MARCH HARE: (in an encouraging tone) Have some wine.

ALICE: (looking down the table) I don't see any wine.

MARCH HARE: There isn't any.

ALICE: (angrily) It wasn't very civil of you to offer it.

MARCH HARE: It wasn't very civil of you to sit down without being invited.

ALICE: I didn't know it was *your* table. It's laid for a great many more than three.

HATTER: (to Alice) Your hair wants cutting.

ALICE: (severely) You should learn not to make personal remarks. It's very rude.

HATTER: (opening his eyes very wide) Why is a raven like a writing desk?

ALICE: (to herself) Hmm. Come, we shall have some fun now! I'm glad they've begun asking riddles. (to the Hatter) I believe I can guess that.

MARCH HARE: Do you mean that you think you can find out the answer to it?

ALICE: Exactly so.

MARCH HARE: Then you should say what you mean.

ALICE: I do. At least—at least I mean what I say—that's the same thing, you know.

HATTER: Not the same thing a bit! Why you might just as well say that "I see what I eat" is the same thing as "I eat what I see!"

MARCH HARE: You might just as well say that "I like what I get" is the same thing as "I get what I like!"

DORMOUSE: (talking in his sleep) You might just as well say that "I breathe when I sleep" is the same thing as "I sleep when I breathe!"

HATTER: Dormouse, it is the same with you. (then to Alice) What day of the month is it? I think my pocket watch is not working. (He appears to shake a pocket watch and then hold it to his ears.)

ALICE (thoughtfully) The fourth.

HATTER: (sighing) Two days wrong! I told you butter wouldn't suit the works! (looking angrily at the March Hare)

MARCH HARE: (meekly) It was the *best* butter.

HATTER: Yes, but some crumbs must have got in as well. You shouldn't have put it in with the bread-knife.

MARCH HARE: It was the *best* butter, you know.

ALICE: What a funny watch! It tells the day of the month, and doesn't tell what o'clock it is!

HATTER: Why should it? Does *your* watch tell you what year it is?

ALICE: Of course not, but that's because it stays the same year for such a long time together.

HATTER: Which is just the case with *mine*.

ALICE: (puzzled) I don't quite understand you.

HATTER: (to Alice) Have you guessed the riddle yet?

ALICE: No, I give up. What's the answer?

HATTER: I haven't the slightest idea.

MARCH HARE: Nor I.

ALICE: (sighing wearily) I think you might do something better with the time than wasting it in asking riddles that have no answers.

HATTER: If you knew Time as well as I do, you wouldn't talk about wasting *it*. It's *him*.

ALICE: I don't know what you mean.

HATTER: (contemptuously) Of course you don't! I dare say you never even spoke of Time!

ALICE: (cautiously) Perhaps not, but I know I have to beat time when I learn music.

HATTER: Ah! That accounts for it. He will not stand beating. Now, if you only kept on good terms with him, he'd do almost anything you liked with the clock. For instance, suppose it were nine o'clock in the morning, just time to begin lessons. You'd only have to whisper a hint to Time, and round goes the clock in a twinkling! Half-past one, time for dinner.

MARCH HARE: (to itself in a whisper) I only wish it was.

ALICE: (thoughtfully) That would be grand, certainly, but then—I shouldn't be hungry for it, you know.

HATTER: Not at first, perhaps, but you could keep it to half-past one as long as you liked.

ALICE: Is that the way *you* manage?

HATTER: (mournfully) Not I! We quarreled last March—just before *he* went mad, you know—(pointing at the March Hare)—it was at the great concert given by the Queen of Hearts, and I had to sing

>Twinkle, twinkle, little bat!
>
>How I wonder what you're at!

You know the song, perhaps?

ALICE: I've heard something like it.

HATTER: It goes on, you know, in this way:

>Up above the world you fly,
>
>Like a tea tray in the sky.
>
>Twinkle, twinkle—

DORMOUSE: (shaking itself, but still asleep) Twinkle, twinkle, twinkle, twinkle—

HATTER: Well, I'd hardly finished the first verse when the Queen bawled out, "He's murdering the time! Off with his head!"

ALICE: How dreadfully savage!

HATTER: And ever since that he will not do a thing I ask! It's always six o'clock now.

ALICE: Is that the reason so many tea-things are put out here?

HATTER: (sighing) Yes, that's it. It's always tea-time, and we've no time to wash the things between whiles.

ALICE: Then you keep moving round, I suppose?

HATTER: Exactly so as the things get used up.

ALICE: But what happens when you come to the beginning again?

MARCH HARE: (yawning) Suppose we change the subject. I'm getting tired of this. I vote the young lady tells us a story.

ALICE: (rather alarmed) I'm afraid I don't know one.

HATTER and MARCH HARE: (together) Then the Dormouse shall. Wake up, Dormouse.

DORMOUSE: (in a hoarse and feeble voice) I wasn't asleep. I heard every word you fellows were saying.

MARCH HARE: Tell us a story!

ALICE: Yes, please do!

HATTER: And be quick about it, or you'll be asleep again before it's done.

DORMOUSE: Once upon a time there were three little sisters, and their names were Elsie, Lacie, and Tillie. They lived at the bottom of a well—

ALICE: What did they live on?

DORMOUSE: They lived on treacle.

ALICE: They couldn't have done that, you know. They'd have been ill.

DORMOUSE: So they were. *Very* ill.

ALICE: But why did they live at the bottom of a well?

MARCH HARE: (earnestly) Take some more tea.

ALICE: I've had nothing yet so I can't take more.

HATTER: You mean you can't take *less*. It's very easy to take *more* than nothing.

ALICE: Nobody asked *your* opinion.

HATTER: (triumphantly) Who's making personal remarks now?

ALICE: Dormouse, why did they live at the bottom of a well?

DORMOUSE: (thoughtfully) It was a treacle-well.

ALICE: (angrily) There's no such thing!

HATTER and
MARCH HARE: (together) Sh! Sh!

DORMOUSE: (sulkily) If you can't be civil, you'd better finish the story for yourself.

ALICE: (very humbly) No, please go on! I won't interrupt you again. I dare say there may be *one*.

DORMOUSE: (indignantly) One, indeed! And so these three little sisters—they were learning to draw, you know—

ALICE: (interrupting again) What did they draw? (more cautiously) But I don't understand. Where did they draw the treacle from?

HATTER: You can draw water out of a water-well so I should think you could draw treacle out of a treacle-well—eh, stupid?

ALICE: But, Dormouse, they were *in* the well.

DORMOUSE: Of course they were, well in. They were learning to draw. (yawning and rubbing its eyes) And they drew all manner of things—everything that begins with an *M*—

ALICE: Why with an *M*?

MARCH HARE: Why not?

DORMOUSE: (appearing to doze off and then wake up)—that begins with an *M*, such as mousetraps, and the moon, and memory, and muchness—you know you say things are "much of a muchness"—did you ever see such a thing as a drawing of a muchness?

ALICE: (very much confused) Really, now you ask me. I don't think—

HATTER: Then you shouldn't talk.

NARRATOR: This piece of rudeness is more than Alice can bear. She gets up in great disgust and walks off. The Dormouse falls asleep instantly, and neither of the others takes the least notice of her going, though she looks back once or twice, half hoping that they will call after her. The last time she sees them, they are trying to put the Dormouse into the teapot.

ALICE: At any rate I'll never go *there* again! It's the stupidest tea-party I ever was at in all my life!

NARRATOR: However, this tea-party is no stranger than any other of Alice's adventures in wonderland.

SCRIPTING NOTES:

1. Alice's thoughts are presented as though she is talking out loud to herself.

2. Because the conversation jumps unexpectedly from one character to another, it is necessary to provide extra clues for the listening audience (e.g., by beginning lines by addressing particular characters and by providing stage directions indicating who is being addressed).

3. References to most movement are omitted, although some are written into either stage instructions or dialogue.

A CHRISTMAS CAROL

Charles Dickens

This script is taken from stave 1, "Marley's Ghost." In this scene Marley's Ghost visits Ebenezer Scrooge in his apartment.

STAGING:

The narrator stands at a lectern. The Ghost sits on a stool, and Scrooge sits in a chair.

                    Scrooge   Ghost
                       X   X

        Narrator
           X

NARRATOR: We have chosen to share a scene from *A Christmas Carol* by Charles Dickens. The characters in this scene are Ebenezer Scrooge, read by _____, and Jacob Marley's Ghost, read by _____. I, _____, am the narrator.

Marley, though now dead, had been Scrooge's business partner. As partners, Marley and Scrooge were well matched; both lived only to make a profit. Now, however, Marley's Ghost has a debt to pay. Because in life Marley's spirit never left the counting house, his Ghost must wander far and wide to convince others that the true business of humankind is love, mercy, and patience.

As this scene opens on Christmas Eve, the Ghost bursts through Scrooge's cellar door and stands before him to deliver a message and a warning. Scrooge cannot believe his eyes.

SCROOGE: Humbug! It's humbug still! I won't believe it. (pausing, and then with great surprise) I know him! Marley's Ghost! (coldly demanding) How now! What do you want with me?

GHOST: Much!

SCROOGE: Who are you?

GHOST: Ask me who I *was*.

SCROOGE: (raising his voice) Who *were* you then? You're particular—for a ghost.

GHOST: In life I was your partner, Jacob Marley. You don't believe in me.

SCROOGE: I don't.

GHOST: What evidence would you have of my reality, beyond that of your senses?

SCROOGE: (afraid, yet trying to be clever) Because a little thing affects them. You may be an undigested bit of beef, a blot of mustard, a crumb of cheese, a fragment of an underdone potato. There's more of gravy than of grave about you, whatever you are! Humbug, I tell you—humbug!

NARRATOR: At this, the Ghost raises a frightful cry, shakes his chain, and then removes the bandage from around his head. Without the bandage, his lower jaw drops upon his chest.

SCROOGE: (with great fear) Mercy! Dreadful apparition, why do you trouble me?

GHOST: Man of the worldly mind! Do you believe in me or not?

SCROOGE: I do. I must. But why do spirits walk the earth, and why do they come to me?

GHOST: It is required of every man that the spirit within him should walk abroad among his fellow-men, and travel far and wide. If that spirit goes not forth in life, it is condemned to do so after death. It is doomed to wander through the world—oh, woe is me!—and witness what it cannot share, but might have shared on earth, and turned to happiness!

SCROOGE: You are wearing a chain. Tell me why?

GHOST: I wear the chain I forged in life. I made it link by link, and yard by yard. I girded it on of my own free will, and of my own free will I wore it. Is its pattern strange to *you*?

SCROOGE: (trembling)

GHOST: Or would you know the weight and length of the strong coil you bear yourself? It was as heavy and as long as this when we were partners. You have laboured on it since. It is a ponderous chain.

SCROOGE: Jacob, old Jacob Marley, tell me more. Speak comfort to me, Jacob.

GHOST: I have none to give. It comes from other regions, Ebenezer Scrooge, and is conveyed by other ministers, to other kinds of men. Nor can I tell you what I would. A very little more is all permitted to me. I cannot rest; I cannot stay; I cannot linger anywhere. My spirit never walked beyond our counting house. Mark me! In life my spirit never roved beyond the narrow limits of our money-changing hole; and weary journeys lie before me!

SCROOGE: (in deep thought) You must have been very slow about it, Jacob.

GHOST: Slow!

SCROOGE: (businesslike, but polite) Seven years dead, and travelling all this time?

GHOST: The whole time. No rest, no peace. Incessant torture of remorse.

SCROOGE: You travel fast?

GHOST: On the wings of the wind.

SCROOGE: You might have got over a great quantity of ground in seven years.

GHOST: Ohhhh! Oh! I was a captive. I was bound, and double-chained when I passed into eternity before I learned the value of goodness. Any Christian spirit working kindly in its little sphere, whatever it may be, will find its mortal life too short for its vast means of usefulness. When I lived I did not know that no space of regret can make amends for one life's opportunities misused! I lived an empty life, and now I can only regret that empty life.

SCROOGE: (trying to follow the Ghost's argument) But you were always a good man of business, Jacob.

GHOST: Business! Mankind was my business. The common welfare was my business; charity, mercy, forbearance, and benevolence, were, all, my business. The dealings of my trade were but a drop of water in the comprehensive ocean of my business! At this time of the year—Christmas—I suffer most. Why did I walk through crowds of fellow beings with my eyes turned down, and never raise them to that blessed Star which led the Wise Men to a poor abode? Were there no poor homes to which its light would have conducted *me*!

SCROOGE: (begins to shake)

GHOST: Hear me! My time is nearly gone.

SCROOGE: I will, but don't be hard upon me! Don't be flowery, Jacob! Pray!

GHOST: How it is that I appear before you in a shape that you can see, I may not tell. I have sat invisible beside you many and many a day.

SCROOGE: (wipes perspiration from his brow)

GHOST: That is no light part of my penance. I am here tonight to warn you, that you have yet a chance and hope of escaping my fate. A chance and hope of my procuring, Ebenezer.

SCROOGE: You were always a good friend to me. Thank you.

GHOST: You will be haunted by Three Spirits.

SCROOGE: (clearly unhappy to hear the prediction) Is that the chance and hope you mentioned, Jacob?

GHOST: It is.

SCROOGE: I—I think I'd rather not.

GHOST: Without their visits you cannot hope to shun the path I tread. Expect the first tomorrow, when the bell tolls one.

SCROOGE: (attempting to bargain) Couldn't I take 'em all at once, and have it over, Jacob?

GHOST: Expect the second on the next night at the same hour. The third upon the next night when the last stroke of twelve has ceased to vibrate. Look to see me no more; and look that, for your own sake, you remember what has passed between us!

NARRATOR: With the Ghost's last words, Scrooge is left alone to think about the coming visits of three more ghosts. Those three will reveal themselves in settings of Christmases past, present, and future. Scrooge will have the amazing and painful opportunity to look backward and forward over his life; and yet, he will know that the Ghost's warning carries with it the hope that Scrooge will be able to avoid Marley's unhappy ending.

SCRIPTING NOTES:

1. In one of Scrooge's lines the word "ghost" was used in place of "shade."

2. Most references to movement (walking, sitting, etc.) were omitted.

3. Several exchanges between the Ghost and Scrooge were omitted in order for young listeners to maintain the focus of the encounter.

4. "You are fettered" was changed to "You are wearing a chain."

5. British spellings were retained.

6. Some longer sentences were shortened and adapted.

HANS BRINKER OR THE SILVER SKATES

Mary Mapes Dodge

This script is taken from an early chapter of *Hans Brinker or the Silver Skates* when Hans and Gretel find a friend.

STAGING:

The narrator stands at a lectern. Hans, Gretel, and Hilda sit on stools.

                                        Gretel
                                          X

                        Hans   Hilda
                         X   X

            Narrator
               X

NARRATOR: The following readers theatre script is from an early chapter in *Hans Brinker or the Silver Skates* by Mary Mapes Dodge. The characters are Hans, a poor peasant, who is clever at woodcarving, read by _____; his younger sister Gretel, read by _____; and Hilda, the rich burgomaster's kind daughter, read by _____. I, _____, am the narrator.

On this bright December noon, poorly dressed Hans and Gretel are watching the other skaters after trying to skate on the canal on clumsy pieces of wood carved by Hans and tied with rawhide. Hilda's friends have been making fun of Hans and Gretel, so she skates away and draws up beside Gretel.

HILDA: What is your name, little girl?

GRETEL: It is Gretel, and my brother is called Hans.

HILDA: (cheerily) Hans is a stout fellow and seems to have a warm stove somewhere within him, but you look cold. You should wear more clothing, little one.

GRETEL: (trying to laugh) I am not so very little. I am past twelve years old.

HILDA: Oh, I beg your pardon! You see, I am nearly fourteen, and so large for my age that other girls seem small to me. But that is nothing. Perhaps you will shoot up far above me yet. Not unless you dress more warmly, though; shivering girls never grow.

HANS: (sadly) My sister has not complained of the cold; but this is bitter weather and she has nothing else to wear.

GRETEL: (trying to hide her tears) It is nothing, I am often warm, too warm, when I am skating. You are good, miss, to think of it.

HILDA: (angry at herself) No, no! I am careless, cruel; but I meant no harm. I wanted to ask you—I mean—if—

HANS: (interrupting eagerly) What is it, young lady? If there is any service I can do, any—

HILDA: (laughing off her embarrassment) Oh no, no! I only wished to speak to you about the grand race. Why do you not join it? You both can skate well, and the ranks are free. Anyone may enter for the prize of a beautiful pair of silver skates.

HANS: Ah, miss, even if we could enter, we could skate only a few strokes with the rest. Our skates are hard wood, you see, (holding up his foot) but they soon become damp. Then they stick and trip us.

GRETEL: Oh, no! We can't join, but may we be there, my lady, on the great day to look on?

HILDA: (kindly) Which of you is the better skater?

HANS: (promptly) Gretel.

GRETEL: (speaking at the same time as Hans) Hans.

HILDA: (smiling) I wish from my heart that I had not spent so much of my monthly allowance for lace and finery. I cannot buy you each a pair of skates, or even one good pair, as I have only eight small silver coins. Here they are. Decide between you which of you stands the best chance of winning the race and buy the skates accordingly. I wish I had enough to buy better ones. Good-bye, I must rejoin my friends.

HANS: We cannot take this money, though we know your goodness in giving it.

HILDA: (embarrassed) Why not?

HANS: Because we have not earned it.

HILDA: (quickly) Carve me a chain, Hans, like the one your sister wears.

HANS: That I will, lady, with all my heart. We have whitewood in the house fine as ivory. You shall have one tomorrow, but do take back the money.

HILDA: No, no! That sum will be but a poor price for the chain. Now, I must be off.

HANS: It is all right, Gretel. I will work hard every minute, and sit up half the night, if mother will let me burn a candle. The chain shall be finished so we may keep the money, Gretel.

GRETEL: (happily) What a good young lady! Oh, Hans! Was it for nothing the stork settled on our roof last summer? Do you remember how our mother said it would bring us luck and how she cried when Janzoon Kolp shot it? Mother said it would bring him trouble. But the luck has come to us, at last. Now, Hans, if mother sends us to town tomorrow, you can buy the skates in the marketplace.

HANS: (shaking his head) The young lady would have given us the money to buy skates; but if I earn it, Gretel, it shall be spent for wool. You must have a warm jacket.

GRETEL: (dismayed) Oh! Not buy the skates. Why, I am not often cold. Mother says the blood runs up and down in poor children's veins, humming, "I must keep 'em warm; I must keep 'em warm!" Don't say you won't buy the skates; it makes me feel just like crying. Besides, I want to be cold—I mean I'm real, awful warm— so, now! (sobbing)

HANS: Don't cry, Gretel.

GRETEL: I'll feel awful if you give up the skates. I don't want them; I'm not as stingy as that. But I want you to have them; and then, when I get bigger, they'll do for me. Oh, count the pieces of money, Hans. Did you ever see so many?

HANS: (turning the money over in his hand) No, Gretel, I can wait. Some day I may have money enough saved to buy a fine pair. You shall have these.

GRETEL: The young lady gave the money to you, Hans. I'd be real bad to take it.

HANS: I insist. Come, let's take off our wooden "rockers" and hurry home to tell Mother the good news.

GRETEL: Oh, I know. You can do this. You can get a pair of skates a little too small for you, and too big for me, and we can take turns using them.

HANS: Nonsense, Gretel! You could never skate with a big pair. You stumbled about with these wooden ones like a blind chicken before I curved off the ends. No, you must have a pair to fit exactly, and you must practice every chance you can get until the race. My little Gretel shall win the silver skates.

NARRATOR: Hansel earns money for another pair of skates by carving a second necklace. Thus they both can enter the race. Who will win?

SCRIPTING NOTES:

1. In two instances Hans was given additional explanation as part of his speech in order to avoid the need of a narrator explanation.

2. The word "miss" was used as a translation of *jufvrouw*. Small silver coins is the translation used for *kwartje*.

"ONE-EYE, TWO-EYES, AND THREE-EYES"

Jacob and Wilhelm Grimm

The following script is taken from the opening scene where Two-Eyes discovers a way to find food. This story is from *Grimm's Household Tales.*

STAGING:

The narrator stands at a lectern. Two-Eyes sits on the floor. The wise woman sits near her on a low stool. The mother and the other two sisters sit in chairs.

One-Eye
X

Mother   Two-Eyes   Wise Woman
X   X   X

Three-Eyes
X

Narrator
X

NARRATOR: We shall share with you the opening scenes from "One-Eye, Two-Eyes, and Three-Eyes," a tale collected by the Brothers Grimm. The characters include Two-Eyes, a mistreated, gentle girl, read by _____; her cruel mother, read by _____; her two mean sisters, Three-Eyes and One-Eye, who do everything they can to make Two-Eyes unhappy, read by _____ and _____; and the wise woman who helps Two-Eyes, read by _____. I, _____, am the narrator.

The three daughters are named One-Eye, Two-Eyes, and Three-Eyes because that is how many eyes each one has. Two-eyes sees just as most people do, so her mother and two sisters cannot endure her.

MOTHER: (scornfully) You, with your two eyes are no better than the common people. You do not belong to us!

NARRATOR: They push Two-Eyes about, give her rags to wear and little to eat, so she goes hungry to the field to tend the goat. She can bear it no longer, so she sits down on the ridge and begins to weep bitterly. Suddenly, a woman is beside her.

WISE WOMAN: (kindly) Why are you weeping, little Two-Eyes?

TWO-EYES: (sadly) Have I not reason to weep, when I have two eyes like other people, and my sisters and mother hate me for it? They push me from one corner to another, throw old clothes at me, and give me nothing to eat but the scraps they leave. Today they have given me so little that I am still quite hungry. (weeps bitterly)

WISE WOMAN: Wipe away your tears, Two-Eyes, and I will tell you something to stop you from ever suffering from hunger again.

TWO-EYES: (ceasing her crying) What can I do?

WISE WOMAN: Just say to your goat,

> Bleat, my little goat, bleat,
> Cover the table with something to eat.

Then a clean well-spread table will stand before you, with the most delicious food upon it of which you may eat as much as you like. When you have had enough, and have no more need of the little table, just say,

> Bleat, bleat, my little goat, I pray,
> And take the table quite away.

Then it will vanish from your sight.

NARRATOR: Then, the wise woman departs.

TWO-EYES: (excited) I must instantly try to see if what she said is true, for I am far too hungry.

> Bleat, my little goat, bleat,
> Cover the table with something to eat.

NARRATOR: As soon as Two-Eyes speaks the words, a little table is standing before her covered with the most delicious food, warm and smoking as if it has just come from the kitchen. Two-Eyes eats until she is satisfied; then she speaks.

TWO-EYES: Bleat, bleat, my little goat, I pray,
And take the table quite away.

NARRATOR: Immediately the little table and everything on it are gone again.

TWO-EYES: (happily) This is a delightful way to keep house!

NARRATOR: For the next three days Two-Eyes does not eat the bits of broken bread her sisters and mother give her, and they are much surprised. Finally, they plot together.

TRHEE-EYES: There is something wrong about Two-Eyes. She always leave her food untasted, and she used to eat up everything that was given her.

ONE-EYE   She must have discovered other ways of getting food. How can we learn the truth?

MOTHER: Tomorrow, One-Eye, when Two-Eyes drives the goat to pasture, you go with her and observe what she does while she is there. See whether anyone brings her anything to eat or drink.

NARRATOR: The next morning, One-Eye addresses Two-Eyes scornfully.

ONE-EYE: I will go with you to the pasture to see that the goat is well taken care of and driven where there is food.

NARRATOR: Two-Eyes knows what One-Eye has in mind, but she is too wise to be tricked, so they drive the goat to the high grass.

TWO-EYES: Come, One-Eye, you are tired after your unaccustomed walk and the heat of the sun. Let's sit down and I'll sing something to you.

ONE-EYE: (haughtily) All right. I think I will lie down and rest a bit. But sing softly, I can't bear your voice.

TWO-EYES: (singing monotonously)

   One-Eye, wakest thou?

   One-Eye, sleepest thou?

(pauses and looks at One-Eye, then continues)

   One-Eye, wakest thou?

   One-Eye, sleepest thou?

(Looking closely at One-Eye) Aha, you are fast asleep, now I can eat and you won't see me.

   Bleat, my little goat, bleat,

  Cover the table with something to eat.

NARRATOR: After Two-Eyes has eaten her fill, she says the magic words and the table disappears. Then she awakens One-Eye.

TWO-EYES: One-Eye, you are not able to care for the goat. You go to sleep while you are doing it, and in the meantime the little goat might run all over the world.

ONE-EYE: (angrily) Be quiet. Let us go home.

NARRATOR: They go home and again, Two-Eyes leaves her scraps of food untouched. Three-Eyes and her mother can hardly wait to hear One-Eye's story of the day.

THREE-EYES: Two-Eyes is still not hungry. Tell us why she didn't eat, One-Eye.

MOTHER: Yes, tell us what happened.

ONE-EYE: I fell asleep when I was out.

MOTHER: You foolish girl! Tomorrow, Three-Eyes, you shall go and observe if Two-Eyes eats anything when she is out. Watch carefully and see if anyone fetches her food and drink. She must be eating and drinking in secret.

THREE-EYES: All right. Tomorrow I will find out the truth.

NARRATOR: Three-Eyes does go with Two-Eyes the next day. Will she see what happens, or will she too fall asleep?

SCRIPTING NOTES:

1. Terms such as "dost" and "mayst" were changed to "do" and "may."

2. The description that could have been assigned to the narrator has been shortened so that the narrator does not dominate the script.

"THE WATER OF LIFE"

Jacob and Wilhelm Grimm

The following script is taken from the opening scene where the brothers try to find a way to cure their father. This story is from *Grimm's Household Tales*.

STAGING:

The narrator stands at a lectern. The old man and the sons sit in chairs. The King sits in an arm chair and the dwarf sits on the floor.

King
X

Eldest Son
X

Middle Son   Dwarf
X   X

Youngest Son
X

Old Man
X

Narrator
X

NARRATOR: We shall share with you the opening scenes from "The Water of Life," a tale collected by the Brothers Grimm. The characters include the very ill King, read by _____; the old man who suggests a cure, read by _____; the little dwarf who works magic, read by _____; the King's kind, honest, youngest son, read by _____; the selfish middle son, read by _____; and the haughty eldest son, read by _____. I, _____, am the narrator.

    The King is very ill, and no one believes that he can recover. His three sons are very distressed. They go into the palace garden, and as they are weeping, an old man appears.

OLD MAN: (kindly) What is the cause of your grief?

YOUNGEST SON: (sadly) Our father, the King, is so ill that he will most certainly die, for nothing seems to cure him.

OLD MAN: I know of one more remedy and that is the water of life. If he drinks of it he will become well again, but it is hard to find.

ELDEST SON: I shall go and tell the King that I know of a cure and I will manage to find it.

NARRATOR:	So saying, the eldest son goes to the King's bedroom.
ELDEST SON:	Father, an old man in the garden told us about the water of life, which is hard to find but will certainly cure you. Please, may I go forth and search for it?
KING:	No, the danger is too great. I would rather die.
ELDEST SON:	I beg of you, Father, let me go forth, I am not afraid.
NARRATOR:	The eldest son begs so hard that the King consents. The eldest son is delighted. He thinks that if he brings the water, he will be the King's favored son and inherit the kingdom. He sets out and has ridden only a short distance when he sees a dwarf in the road.
DWARF:	Where are you going at such a fast pace?
ELDEST SON:	(haughtily) Out of my way, you silly shrimp. It is nothing to you, and I must hurry on.
DWARF:	(angrily) Ride on, fool. (pause) Aha, you are out of sight and I can now cast an evil spell. Soon you will enter a ravine, and the farther you ride, the closer the mountains will draw together. At last the road will become so narrow that you will be unable to advance a step farther. It will be impossible either for you to turn your horse or to dismount from the saddle. You will be shut in as if in prison.
NARRATOR:	The spell cast by the dwarf happens just as the dwarf states it, and the King waits in vain for the return of his eldest son.
KING:	I fear your brother is lost and we will never see him again.
MIDDLE SON:	Father, let me go forth to seek the water of life.
KING:	No, son, I would rather die than lose you also.
MIDDLE SON:	Please, Father, I shall take care, and I will return.
NARRATOR:	At last, the King yields and the middle son sets out on the same road, thinking that if the eldest son were dead, the kingdom will fall to him. Soon he meets the dwarf.
DWARF:	Where are you going in such haste?
MIDDLE SON:	Out of my way, little shrimp. That is nothing to thee.

DWARF:	Ride on then. (pause) Yes, you are now out of sight. I shall bewitch you like the other. When you get into the ravine, you will be able neither to go forward nor backward. So fare haughty people.
NARRATOR:	As the middle son also remains away, the youngest begs to be allowed to go forth to fetch the water. At last the King is obliged to let him go. The youngest son also soon meets the dwarf.
DWARF:	Where are you going in such haste?
YOUNGEST SON:	I am seeking the water of life, for my father is sick and will surely die if I do not find it.
DWARF:	Do you know, then, where the water is to be found?
YOUNGEST SON:	No.
DWARF:	Since you have answered in a kindly way and not haughtily like your false brothers, I will give you the information and tell you how you may obtain the water of life.
YOUNGEST SON:	Is it far from here?
DWARF:	It springs from a fountain in the courtyard of an enchanted castle. You will not be able to make your way to it, however, if I do not give you an iron wand and two small loaves of bread. Strike three times with the wand on the iron door of the castle and it will spring open. Inside lie two lions with gaping jaws, but if you throw a loaf to each of them, they will be quieted. Hasten to fetch some of the water of life before the clock strikes twelve or the door will shut again, and you will be imprisoned.
YOUNGEST SON:	Thank you so much for the wand and bread. Now I must be on my way.
NARRATOR:	Even with the dwarf's help, the youngest son faces great danger. Through his kindness in rescuing his treacherous older brothers, he almost loses his own life *and* the love of his father. However, good does triumph in the end.

SCRIPTING NOTES:

1. In order to aid understanding, words such as "whither" and "thou" were changed to "where" and "you."

2. To avoid confusion, the thoughts of the two brothers were incorporated into the narrator's lines.

"HOW THE CAMEL GOT HIS HUMP"

Rudyard Kipling

This tale is taken from the *Just So Stories for Little Children.*

STAGING:

The narrator stands at a lectern. The Djinn sits on a tall stool. The Camel stands. The Horse, the Dog, and the Ox sit in chairs, and the Man sits on the floor.

		Horse X	Dog X		
---	Camel X			Ox X	
Djinn X					Man X
Narrator X					

NARRATOR: This readers theatre presentation is from *How the Camel Got His Hump,* a story by Rudyard Kipling. The characters in the story are the magical and powerful Djinn, read by _____; the Camel, read by _____; the Horse, read by _____; the Dog, read by _____; the Ox, read by _____; and the Man, read by _____. I, _____, am the narrator.

In the beginning when the world is so new-and-all, and the Horse, the Dog, and the Ox are just begining to work for Man, there is the Camel. He lives in the middle of a Howling Desert because he does not want to work; and besides, he is a Howler himself. So he eats sticks and thorns and tamarisks and milkweed and prickles, and when anybody speaks to him, he says, "Humph!" Just "Humph!" and no more. One by one the other animals come to him to ask him to do his share of the work.

HORSE: Camel, O Camel, come out and trot like the rest of us.

CAMEL: (rudely) Humph!

HORSE: I shall go tell the Man.

DOG: Camel, O Camel, come and fetch and carry like the rest of us.

CAMEL: Humph!

DOG: I shall go tell the Man.

OX: Camel, O Camel, come and plough like the rest of us.

CAMEL: Humph!

OX: I shall go tell the Man.

NARRATOR: At the end of the day the Man calls the Horse and the Dog and the Ox together.

MAN: Three, O Three, I'm very sorry for you (with the world so new-and-all); but that Humph-thing in the Desert can't work, or he would have been here by now, so I am going to leave him alone, and you must work double time to make up for it.

CAMEL: (laughing) Humph!

NARRATOR: Presently there comes along the Djinn in charge of All Deserts, rolling in a cloud of dust (Djinns always travel that way because it is Magic), and he stops to palaver and pow-pow with the Three.

HORSE: Djinn of All Deserts, *is* it right for any one to be idle, with the world so new-and-all?

DJINN: Certainly not.

HORSE: Well, there's a thing in the middle of your Howling Desert (and he's a Howler himself) with a long neck and long legs, and he hasn't done a stroke of work since Monday morning. He won't trot.

DJINN: Whew! (whistling) That's my Camel, for all the gold in Arabia! What does he say about it?

DOG: He says, "Humph!" and he won't fetch and carry.

DJINN: Does he say anything else?

OX: Only "Humph!"; and he won't plough.

DJINN: Very good. I'll humph him if you will kindly wait a minute. Camel, my friend, what's this I hear of your doing no work, with the world so new-and-all?

CAMEL: Humph!

DJINN: (with his chin in his hand as though thinking) Camel, you've given the Three extra work ever since Monday morning, all on account of your 'scruciating idleness.

CAMEL: Humph!

DJINN: I shouldn't say that again if I were you. You might say it once too often. Camel, I want you to work.

CAMEL: Humph!

NARRATOR: No sooner has Camel said it than he sees his back, that he is so proud of, puffing up and puffing up into a great big lolloping humph.

DJINN: Do you see that hump? That's your very own humph that you've brought upon your very own self by not working. Today is Thursday, and you've done no work since Monday, when the work began. Now you are going to work.

CAMEL: How can I with this humph on my back?

DJINN: That's made a-purpose all because you missed those three days. You will be able to work now for three days without eating, because you can live on your humph; and don't you ever say I never did anything for you. Stay with the Three, and behave.

CAMEL: Humph! Humph!

NARRATOR: From that day to this the Camel always wears a humph. Now we call it "hump" so that we will not hurt his feelings. However, he has never yet caught up with the three days that he missed at the beginning of the world, and he has never yet learned how to behave.

SCRIPTING NOTES:
1. Descriptions of some actions (e.g., that of the Three going to tell the Man) are incorporated into the dialogue.

2. Instead of addressing a pool of water to speak to the Camel, the Djinn speaks directly to the Camel.

3. To avoid movement and shifts in scenes, all the characters are placed in a single setting.

HEIDI

Johanna Spyri

This script is from chapter 1, "Up the Mountain," and from the beginning of chapter 2, "With Grandfather."

STAGING:

The narrator stands at a lectern. The remaining readers sit on stools.

Dete   Heidi

X   X

Barbel   Grandfather

X   X

Narrator

X

NARRATOR: The script that we have chosen to share is from *Heidi* by Johanna Spyri. The characters in this scene are five-year-old Heidi, read by _____; Dete, her heartless aunt, read by _____; Heidi's hermit-like grandfather, read by _____; and Barbel, a village gossip, read by _____. Dete is now taking Heidi, an orphan, to live on the mountain with Grandfather whom the villagers know as Uncle. Along the way she explains the family history to Barbel who has joined the pair. I, _____, am the narrator.

DETE: Are you tired, Heidi?

HEIDI: No, I am hot.

DETE: (encouragingly) We shall soon get to the top now. You must walk bravely on a little longer, and take good long steps, and in another hour we shall be there.

BARBEL: And where are you off to with the child? I suppose it is the child your sister left?

DETE: Yes. I am taking her up to Uncle, where she must stay.

BARBEL: (shocked) The child stay up there with Alm-Uncle! You must be out of your senses, Dete! How can you think of such a thing! The old man, however, will soon send you and your proposal packing off home again!

DETE: He cannot very well do that, seeing that he is her grandfather. He must do something for her. I have had the charge of the child till now, and I can tell you, Barbel, I am not going to give up the chance which has just fallen to me of getting a good place, for her sake. It is for the grandfather now to do his duty by her.

BARBEL:	(warmly) That would be all very well if he were like other people, but you know what he is. And what can he do with a child, especially with one so young! The child cannot possibly live with him. But where are you thinking of going yourself?
DETE:	To Frankfurt, where an extra good place awaits me. The people I am going to were down at the hotel last summer, and it was part of my duty to attend upon their rooms. They would have liked then to take me away with them, but I could not leave. Now they are there again and have repeated their offer, and I intend to go with them. You may make up your mind to that!
BARBEL:	(with horrified pity) I am glad I am not the child! Not a creature knows anything about the old man up there! He will have nothing to do with anybody, and never sets his foot inside a church from one year's end to another. When he does come down once in a while, everybody clears out of the way of him and his big stick. The mere sight of him, with his bushy grey eyebrows and his immense beard, is alarming enough.
DETE:	Well, and what of that? He is the grandfather all the same, and must look after the child. He is not likely to do her any harm, and if he does, *he* will be answerable for it, not I.
BARBEL:	(full of reproach) It surprises me beyond words that you can think of doing such a thing, Dete.
DETE:	What do you mean? I have done my duty by the child, and what would you have me do with it now? I cannot certainly take a child of five years old with me to Frankfurt. But where are you going, Barbel? We are now halfway up the mountain.
BARBEL:	We have just reached the place I wanted. I had something to say to the goatherd's wife, who does some spinning for me in the winter. So good-bye, Dete, and good luck to you!
NARRATOR:	Dete and Heidi continue climbing up the mountainside, and about an hour later they reach the grandfather's hut, which stands on the top of the mountain. When they clamber into view, Grandfather is sitting on a bench next to his hut. He is quietly looking out over the valley below.
HEIDI:	Good-evening, Grandfather.
GRANDFATHER:	(gruffly) So, so, what is the meaning of this?

DETE: I wish you good-day, Uncle, and I have brought you your grandchild. You will hardly recognize her, as you have not seen her since she was a year old.

GRANDFATHER: (curtly) And what has the child to do with me up here?

DETE: The child is here to remain with you. I have, I think, done my duty by her for these four years, and now it is time for you to do yours.

GRANDFATHER: That's it, is it? And when the child begins to fret and whine after you, as is the way with these unreasonable little beings, what am I to do with her then?

DETE: That's your problem. I know I had to put up with her without complaint when she was left on my hands as an infant, and with enough to do as it was for my mother and self. Now I have to go and look after my own earnings, and you are the next of kin to the child. If you cannot arrange to keep her, do with her as you like. You will be answerable for the result if harm happens to her. However, you have hardly need to add to the burden already on your conscience.

GRANDFATHER: (commanding Dete) Be off with you this instant, and get back as quickly as you can to the place whence you came, and do not let me see your face again in a hurry.

DETE: (quickly) Good-bye to you then, and to you, too, Heidi.

GRANDFATHER: Heidi, what is it you want?

HEIDI: I want to see what you have inside the house.

GRANDFATHER: Come then! Bring your bundle of clothes in with you.

NARRATOR: Thus Heidi begins her life with Grandfather, and the days that follow are far different from the ones that Barbel has predicted.

SCRIPTING NOTES:

1. Less familiar terms and places were changed to more familiar ones. For example,"hotel" was used in place of the "Baths at Ragatz," and "mountain" was used in place of "Alm Mountain."

2. The lengthy explanations of Grandfather's family, of Heidi's losing her clothes, and of their encounter with the goatherd were omitted.

3. References to Heidi's parents, Tobias and Adelaide, were omitted.

4. Except for the narrator's comments, references to movement were omitted.

TREASURE ISLAND
Robert Louis Stevenson

This script is from chapter 11, "What I Heard in the Apple-Barrel."

STAGING:

The narrator stands at a lectern. The remaining readers sit on stools; however, Israel Hands is not present until after Long John Silver whistles for him. An empty barrel sits off to the side; the audience is told that it is the hiding place of Jim Hawkins.

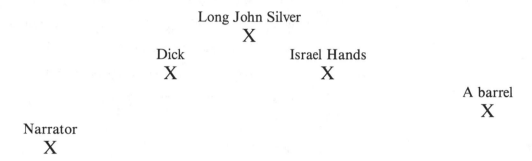

		Long John Silver		
		X		
	Dick		Israel Hands	
	X		X	
				A barrel
				X
Narrator				
X				

NARRATOR: This scene is from Robert Louis Stevenson's novel *Treasure Island*. The main character of the novel is Jim Hawkins; however, in this scene he is quietly hidden away in an apple-barrel as he overhears plans of mutiny aboard the *Hispaniola*. Therefore, he does not speak or show himself. The three readers, all pirates or "gentlemen of fortune," are Long John Silver, read by _____; the youngest seaman, Dick, read by _____; and, appearing later in the scene, Israel Hands, read by _____. I, _____, am the narrator.

Young Jim Hawkins is sailing from Bristol, England, to Treasure Island. This great adventure began after Jim found a treasure map in the bottom of an old pirate's sea chest. The map was shared with trusted men who set about to hire a ship and a crew; unfortunately, a pirate, Long John Silver, came aboard as the ship's cook. Eavesdropping from inside an apple barrel, Jim now discovers Long John Silver's planned mutiny, his true motive for signing on the *Hispaniola*. Jim hears Silver's voice first, and, before a dozen words are spoken, decides he can't show himself for the world.

SILVER: (bragging) No, I was not the captain on the early voyages. Flint was the captain. I was quartermaster because of my timber leg. I lost my leg during the skirmish when old Pew lost his eyesight. It was a master surgeon who amputated that leg. He was out of college and all, but he was hanged like a dog, and sun-dried like the rest at Corso Castle. That trip out we sailed the old *Walrus,* Flint's old ship, and I saw that one red with blood and fit to sink with gold.

DICK: Ah! Flint was the best of the pirates.

SILVER: Here is my own story: I sailed first with the pirate England and then with Flint himself. I took a lot of gold with England, and even more with Flint. That ain't bad for a man before the mast—all safe in the bank. The difference in the end is not what you earn but what you save. Where are the other pirates now? I dunno. Why, most of 'em are here on the *Hispaniola,* and glad to get the work. Some of them have been begging until now. Old Pew, who lost his eyesight, spent twelve hundred pounds in a year. He lived like a lord in Parliament. Where is he now? Well, he's dead now; but for two years before that, shiver my timbers (exclamatory tone), the man was starving. He begged, and he stole, and he cut throats, and starved at that, by the powers!

DICK: Well, pirating ain't much use, after all.

SILVER: It isn't much use for fools; you may say that. (attempting to persuade Dick to join the mutiny) But now, you look here: you're young, you are, and you're as smart. (flattering the young seaman) I saw that when I set my eyes on you, and I'll talk to you like a man. Here it is about gentlemen of fortune. They live rough, and they risk hanging, but they eat and drink like fighting-cocks, and when a cruise is done, why it's hundreds of pounds instead of hundreds of farthings in their pockets. Now, the most of them go for rum and a good fling, and to sea again in their shirts. But that's not the course I lay. I save my gold, putting away some here, some there, and none too much anywheres because I'm suspicious. I'm fifty years old, mark you; when I get back home from this cruise I'll live in style as a gentleman. You know it's time, too. Ah, but I've lived easy all these years; I never denied myself anything my heart desired. I slept soft and ate dainty all my days except when I was cruising. And how did I begin? Before the mast, like you!

DICK: Well, but all the other money's gone now, ain't it? You won't dare show your face in Bristol after this.

SILVER: Why? Where might you suppose the money was?

DICK: At Bristol, in banks and places.

SILVER: It was. It was when we set sail. But my old missis has it all by now. And the

Spy-glass Inn is sold, lease and good-will and all; and the missis is off to meet me. I would tell you where, for I trust you; but it would make jealousy among the mates.

DICK: And can you trust your missis?

SILVER: Gentlemen of fortune usually trust little among themselves, and right they are, you may bet on it. But I have a way with me, I have. There was some that was feared of Pew, and some that was feared of Flint; and Flint his own self was feared of me. Feared he was, and proud. They was the roughest crew afloat, was Flint's; the devil himself would have been feared to go to sea with them. Well, now, I tell you, I'm not a boasting man, and you see how easy I keep company; but when I was quartermaster, lambs wasn't the word for Flint's old buccaneers. Ah, you may be sure of yourself in old John's ship.

DICK: Well, I tell you now, I didn't half a quarter like the job till I had this talk with you, John.

SILVER: And a brave lad you are, and smart, too, and a finer figurehead for a gentleman of fortune I never clapped my eyes on. (Pauses and then gives a little whistle that signals Israel Hands to enter.)

HANDS: (Walks to the stool and sits.)

SILVER: (to Hands) Dick's with us.

HANDS: Oh, I know'd Dick was square. He's no fool, is Dick. But look here, here's what I want to know, Silver: when is this ship ours? I've had almost enough of Captain Smollett; he's hazed me long enough, by thunder! I want to go into that cabin, I do. I want their pickles and wines, and that.

SILVER: Your head ain't much account, not ever was. But you're able to hear, I reckon; leastways, your ears is big enough. Now, here's what I say: you'll berth forward, and you'll live hard, and you'll speak soft, and you'll keep sober, till I give the word; and you may bet on that, my son.

HANDS: Well, I don't say no, do I? What I say is, when? When is this ship ours? That's what I say.

SILVER: Well, now, if you want to know, I'll tell you when. The last moment I can manage; and that's when. Here's a first-rate seaman, Captain Smollett, sails the blessed ship for us. Here's this squire and doctor with a map and such—I don't know where it is, do I? No more do you, says you. Well, then, I mean this squire and doctor shall find the stuff, and help us to get it aboard, by the powers! Then we'll see. If I was sure of you all, sons of double Dutchmen, I'd have Captain Smollett navigate us half-way back again before I struck.

HANDS: Why, we're all seamen aboard here, I should think!

SILVER: (snapping) We can steer a course, but who's to set one? If I had my way I'd have Captain Smollett work us back into favorable winds at least; then we'd have no blessed miscalculations and a spoonful of water a day. But I know the sort you are. I'll finish 'em at the island, as soon's the treasure's on board, and a pity it is. But you're never happy till you're drunk. Slit my sides, I've a sick heart to sail with the likes of you!

HANDS: Easy, Long John. Who's a-crossin' of you?

SILVER: Why, how many tall ships, think ye, now, have I seen lain aboard, and how many brisk lads drying in the sun at Execution Dock? And all for this same hurry and hurry and hurry. You hear me? I seen a thing or two at sea, I have. If you would only lay your course, and point to windward, you would ride in carriages, you would. But not you! I know you. You'll have your mouthful of rum tomorrow, and go hang.

HANDS: Everybody know'd you was a kind of chaplain, Silver; but there's others as could hand and steer as well as you. They liked a bit o' fun, they did. They wasn't so high and dry, nohow, but took their fling, like jolly companions every one.

SILVER: So? Well, and where are they now? Pew was that sort, and died a beggar-man. Flint was, and he died of rum at Savannah. Ah, they was a sweet crew, they was! Only where are they?

DICK: But when we take over, what are we to do with 'em, anyhow?

SILVER: (admiringly) There's the man for me! That's what I call business. Well, what would you think? Put the men ashore like maroons? Or cut 'em down like that much pork?

HANDS: Dead men don't cause trouble.

SILVER: Right you are, rough and ready. But mark you here: I'm an easy man—I'm quite the gentleman, says you; but this time it's serious. Duty is duty, mates. I give my vote—death. I don't want none of these sea-lawyers in the cabin a-coming home, unlooked for, like the devil at prayers. Wait is what I say; but when the time comes, why, let her rip!

HANDS: (shouting) John, you're a man!

SILVER: (fist in the air) To luck! To old Flint! (to himself in a kind of song) Here's to ourselves, and hold your luff, plenty of prizes and plenty of duff.

NARRATOR: At that point a distant voice rings out, "Land, ho." Treasure Island is in sight, and every honest man aboard depends upon Jim Hawkins and Jim Hawkins alone.

SCRIPTING NOTES:

1. Variant names (e.g., "Barbecue" as a nickname for Long John Silver) were not used.

2. Except for the entry of Israel Hands, references to movement were omitted.

3. The scene was abridged.

4. Much of the dialogue was shortened, and less familiar words and phrases were adapted to the needs of contemporary listeners. For example, "eyesight" was used in place of "deadlights," and "amputated" in place of "ampytated."

5. Many references to unknown past pirates and their various ships were omitted.

6. Many of the sailors' more confusing grammatical errors were not included.

REBECCA OF SUNNYBROOK FARM

Kate Douglas Smith Wiggin

This script is taken from chapter 1 as Rebecca goes by stagecoach to live with her aunts.

STAGING:

The narrator stands at a lectern. Mr. Cobb and Rebecca are seated in chairs.

Mr. Cobb   Rebecca

X   X

Narrator

X

NARRATOR: We have chosen to read a scene from *Rebecca of Sunnybrook Farm* by Kate Douglas Wiggin. The characters are the stagecoach driver, Mr. Cobb, read by _____, and fun-loving Rebecca, read by _____. I, _____, am the narrator.

         Rebecca's family is poor, so her two unmarried aunts invite one of the children to come live with them. They prefer Hannah, the oldest, but Rebecca's mother says she can more easily spare Rebecca. Strict Aunt Miranda now feels as though her sister is palming off a wild one on them, but Rebecca is on her way.

         After finding the stagecoach ride a bumpy one, Rebecca asks Mr. Cobb, the stagecoach driver, if she can ride outside with him. He agrees, so now she is visiting with him as they proceed on the trip. She has just explained how each of the seven children in the family was named.

REBECCA: (seriously) I think that's all there is to tell about us.

MR. COBB: (impressed) Land O'Liberty! I should think it was enough. There wasn't many names left when your mother got through choosin'! You've got a powerful good memory! I guess it ain't no trouble for you to learn your lessons, is it?

REBECCA: Not much; the trouble is to get the shoes so I can go and learn 'em. These are spandy new I've got on, and they have to last six months. Mother always says to save my shoes. There don't seem to be any way of saving shoes but taking 'em off and going barefoot; but I can't do that in Riverboro without shaming Aunt Mirandy. I'm going to school right along now when I'm living with Aunt Mirandy, and in two years I'm going to the seminary in Wareham. Mother says it ought to be the making of me! I'm going to be a painter like Miss Ross when

I get through school. At any rate, that's what I think I'm going to be. Mother thinks I'd better teach.

MR. COBB: Your farm ain't the old Hobbs place, is it?

REBECCA: No, it's just Randall's Farm—at least, that's what Mother calls it. I call it Sunnybrook Farm.

MR. COBB: I guess it don't make no difference what you call it so long as you know where it is.

REBECCA: (reproachfully) Oh! Don't say that and be like the rest! It does make a difference what you call things. When I say Randall's Farm, do you see how it looks?

MR. COBB: (uneasily) No, I can't say I do.

REBECCA: Now, when I say Sunnybrook Farm, what does it make you think of?

MR. COBB: (timidly) I suppose there's a brook somewheres near it.

REBECCA: (encouragingly) That's pretty good. You're warm but not hot. There's a brook, but not a common brook. It has young trees and baby bushes on each side of it, and it's a shallow chattering little brook with a white sandy bottom and lots of little shiny pebbles. Whenever there's a bit of sunshine the brook catches it, and it's always full of sparkles the livelong day. Don't your stomach feel hollow? Mine does! I was so afraid I'd miss the stage I couldn't eat any breakfast.

MR. COBB: You'd better have your lunch then. I don't eat nothin' till I get to Milltown. Then I get a piece of pie and a cup of coffee.

REBECCA: I wish I could see Milltown. I suppose it's bigger and grander even than Wareham; more like Paris. Miss Ross told me about Paris. She bought my pink sunshade there and my bead purse. You see how it opens with a snap? I've twenty cents in it, and it's got to last three months for stamps and paper and ink. Mother says Aunt Mirandy won't want to buy things like those when she's feeding and clothing me and paying for my school books.

MR. COBB: (without enthusiasm) Paris ain't so great. It's the dullest place in the State of Maine. I've drove there many a time.

REBECCA: (sternly) Paris is the capital of France, and you have to go to it on a boat. It's in my geography, and it says "The French are a happy and polite people, fond of dancing and light wines." I asked the teacher what light wines were, and he thought it was something like new cider, or maybe ginger pop. I can see Paris as plain as day by just shutting my eyes. The beautiful ladies are always gayly dancing around wth pink sunshades and bead purses, and the grand gentlemen are politely dancing and drinking ginger pop. But you can see Milltown every day with your eyes wide open.

MR. COBB: (shaking his head) Milltown ain't so great, neither. Now you just watch me heave this newspaper right on Miss Brown's doorstep.

REBECCA: (enthusiastically) Oh, how splendid that was! Just like the knife-thrower Mark saw at the circus. I wish there were a long, long row of houses each with a cornhusk mat and a screendoor in the middle, and a newspaper to throw on every one!

MR. COBB: (proudly) I might fail on some of them, you know. If your Aunt Mirandy'll let you, I'll take you down to Milltown some day this summer when the stage ain't full.

REBECCA: (happily) Oh, it can't be true! To think I should see Milltown. It's like having a fairy godmother who asks you your wish and gives it to you! Did you ever read "Cinderella" or "The Yellow Dwarf" or "The Enchanted Frog"?

MR. COBB: (slowly) No, I don't seem to think I ever did read just those particular ones. Where'd you get a chance at so much readin'?

REBECCA: (casually) Oh, I've read lots of books. Father's and Miss Ross's and all the different school teachers', and all in the Sunday School library. I've read *The Lamplighter* and *Ivanhoe* and *David Copperfield* and *Pilgrim's Progress* and lots more. What have you read?

MR. COBB: I've never happened to read those particular books. But land! I've read a sight in my time. Nowdays I'm so drove I get along with the *Almanac,* the *Weekly Argus* and the *Main State Agriculturist.* There's the river again. This is the last long hill, and when we git to the top of it we'll see the chimbleys of Riverboro in the distance. It ain't fur. I live 'bout half a mile beyond your aunts' brick house myself.

REBECCA: (nervously) I didn't think I was going to be afraid, but I guess I am when you say it's coming so near.

MR. COBB: (curiously) Would you go back?

REBECCA: (proudly) I'd never go back. I might be frightened, but I'd be ashamed to run. Going to Aunt Mirandy's is like going down to the cellar in the dark. There might be ogres and giants under the stairs—but, as I tell Hannah, there *might* be elves and fairies and enchanted frogs! Is there a main street in the village like there is in Wareham?

MR. COBB: I s'pose you might call it a main street, an' your Aunt Sawyer lives on it; but there ain't no stores nor mills, an' it's an awful one-horse village! You have to go 'cross the river an' get to our side if you want to see anything goin' on.

REBECCA: (sighing) I'm almost sorry because it would be so grand to drive down a real main street, sitting high up like this behind two splendid horses with my pink sunshade up and everybody in town wondering who the bunch of lilacs and the hair trunk belongs to. It would be just like the beautiful lady in the circus parade we saw last summer.

MR. COBB: There ain't no harm, as I can see, in our makin' the grand entry in the biggest style we can. I'll take the whip out, set up straight, an' drive fast. You hold your bo'quet in your lap, an' open your little red parasol, an' we'll just make the natives stare!

REBECCA: (sadly) I forgot—Mother put me inside, and maybe she'd want me to be there when I got to Aunt Mirandy's. Maybe I'd be more genteel inside, and then I wouldn't have to be jumped down and my clothes fly up, but could open the door and step down like a lady passenger. Would you please stop a minute, Mr. Cobb, and let me change?

MR. COBB: (good-naturedly) of course. We've had a great trip, and we've got real well acquainted, haven't we? You won't forget about Milltown?

REBECCA: (warmly) Never! And you're sure you won't either?

MR. COBB: (seriously) Never! Cross my heart!

NARRATOR: Thus Rebecca arrives at the brick house to live with quick-tempered Aunt Miranda and timid Aunt Jane. Rebecca has problems with Aunt Miranda's sharp tongue, but the ending shows how both of them change. As Rebecca leans her head against the door, she closes her eyes and whispers "God bless Aunt Miranda; God bless the brick house that was; God bless the brick house that is to be!"

SCRIPTING NOTES:
1. Some of Rebecca's speeches were shortened, e.g., the list of books she had read and the story of the circus parade.

2. Some of Mr. Cobb's colloquial language was changed so it would be easier to read.

3. The action of Mr. Cobb's and Rebecca's getting off the stage at the end of the scene (before the last three speeches) was omitted.

Part III

COMBINING A SET OF SCRIPTS UNDER A COMMON THEME: A READERS THEATRE PROGRAM FEATURING BETSY BYARS

FEATURING A SINGLE THEME

Readers theatre provides an avenue for combining a number of scripts into one program featuring a single theme, which may center on an author, a subject, or a genre. If this approach is used, the purpose of the program should be presented in the narrator's introduction and "tie-ins" may be provided between the titles presented. A narrator, common to all scripts, is the best means of establishing continuity and creating a whole program.

The approach for changing readers depends on the situation and the arrangement of the room. However, one possibility is for the narrator to stand on the left and as the tie-ins between scenes are read by the narrator, the previous readers may quietly leave and the next readers take their places. Any changes in seating arrangement can unobtrusively be made by the new readers. If necessary, the narrator may pause until all the new readers are seated before beginning the introduction of the scene.

The following suggested scripts, all representing books by Betsy Byars, have been developed to provide an example for a thematic program of multiple readers theatre scripts. Usually if an author is used as a theme, the narrator will provide some biographical information that would be particularly relevant to the interest of the audience. If the tie-ins provided in this chapter are not sufficient to satisfy the students' needs, more biographical information can be found in *Something about the Author,* volume 46 (Detroit: Gale Research, 1987), *Something about the Author Autobiography Series,* volume 1 (Detroit: Gale Research, 1986), and *Twentieth Century Children's Writers,* second edition (New York: Macmillan, 1983).

In the case of Betsy Byars, her Newbery-winner, *The Summer of the Swans,* may make a good beginning script. Before the narrator speaks the opening lines, the three characters (Sara, Wanda, and Aunt Willie) will already be on stage. Because all the scripts may not be used in one presentation, it will be necessary to select the appropriate tie-ins. In each script the suggested narrator's opening lines in the single scripts that follow should be adapted by omitting the first sentence and by substituting the tie-in introduction.

Preface the narrator's opening lines to *The Summer of the Swans* with:

Today we have chosen to share a group of scenes from books by Betsy Byars because she is a Newbery-winning author who has written over thirty books for young people. Her books appeal because they are so realistic and usually have their beginnings in something that actually has happened. These initial ideas have come from such sources as newspaper clippings and the experiences of her own children.

Betsy Byars always centers her books on the problems of young people rather than the activities of adults. Her books are fast-moving with entertaining dialogue that is realistic.

We shall begin with her Newbery Award book *The Summer of the Swans.* The idea for this book came from a newspaper report about an old man who was thought to have been lost in the West Virginia mountains. After many people had searched unsuccessfully for him, they found that he had merely become bored with a picnic and had gone home to bed.

PROGRAM TIE-INS

Tie-in for *After the Goat Man:*

Our next scene is taken from *After the Goat Man.* A newspaper story also prompted this book. Many people had been forced to leave their modest West Virginia homes in order for Highway I-79 to be constructed. The picture of one displaced man who kept goats aroused the sympathy of Betsy Byars.

Tie-in for *The House of Wings:*

The idea for *The House of Wings* began with newspaper stories about a flying monster that was frightening local residents. This creature was in reality an injured sandhill crane.

Tie-in for *The Midnight Fox:*

Another of Betsy Byars's stories that involves a genuine concern for animals is *The Midnight Fox.* The sympathetic and protective response of Tommy toward the fox may be the reason that it is one of her favorite books.

Tie-in for *The Cybil War:*

An idea found in *The Cybil War,* but not reflected in the scene we shall present, really happened to one of Betsy Byars's daughters and her close girlfriend many years before the book was written. The two girls tried to drill a hole into the wall between their classrooms so that they could exchange notes. Unfortunately, they were caught by the teacher and sent to the principal's office.

Tie-in for *The Animal, the Vegetable, and John D. Jones:*

In *The Cybil War* two boys are fighting for the attention of Cybil. In contrast, the conflict in *The Animal, the Vegetable, and John D. Jones* results from two sisters' attempts to get rid of John D. Jones.

Tie-in for *Trouble River:*

A different kind of conflict is found in the pioneer story *Trouble River.* Dewey and his grandmother must take a dangerous raft trip to avoid capture.

Tie-in for *Cracker Jackson:*

Instead of a dangerous trip on a raft, in *Cracker Jackson* eleven-year-old Cracker drives his mother's car in an attempt to get his ex-babysitter out of town. The unsuccessful trip does not solve the problem.

Tie-in for *The Blossoms Meet the Vulture Lady:*

Several of Betsy Byars's books revolve around the Blossoms, a poor rural family headed by the grandfather. In *The Blossoms Meet the Vulture Lady* a strange character from the grandfather's past creates an unexpected set of circumstances.

Tie-in for *The Burning Questions of Bingo Brown:*

The last scene in our program today is taken from *The Burning Questions of Bingo Brown.* Bingo has many problems and finding the answers proves difficult.

AFTER THE GOAT MAN

Betsy Byars

This suggested script is taken from the chapter "The Goat Man," in which Figgy tells Harold and Ada that his grandfather is missing.

SUGGESTED STAGING:

The narrator stands at a lectern. Figgy, Harold, and Ada are sitting on the floor.

Ada
X

Harold   Figgy
X   X

Narrator
X

NARRATOR'S OPENING LINES:

The scene we have chosen to read is from *After the Goat Man* by Betsy Byars. The characters are overweight, sensitive, food-loving, exercise-hating Harold, read by _____; Ada, Harold's good friend, read by _____; and fearful Figgy, read by _____. I, _____, am the narrator.

Figgy lives with his eccentric, old grandfather who is called the Goat Man, and they have just moved into one of the new houses built for people displaced by the interstate highway. Grandpa did not want to leave his old cabin. As Ada and Harold wait for Figgy on Ada's porch so they can play Monopoly, they hear on the news that the Goat Man has gone back to his cabin and is threatening to shoot anyone who tries to get him out. However, they do not know that the Goat Man is Figgy's grandfather, as Figgy is a new friend. As the scene opens, Figgy, who wears a rabbit's foot for good luck, finally arrives.

SCRIPTING SUGGESTIONS:

1. Instead of having Harold say, "Well, here comes Figgy at last" to begin the scene, have Harold say: "Well, here you are at last, Figgy." Continue Harold's speech as he tells Ada to get the game out and he'll be banker. These lines allow Figgy to be on stage from the beginning.

2. Be sure to give the reader clues, such as irritably, helplessly, sensitively, etc.

3. After Figgy tells Ada a second time that he cannot play, omit the thoughts of Figgy and continue with Harold's speech in which he assumes that Figgy does not *want* to play.

4. Have Figgy's reader wear a rabbit's foot around his neck so he can finger it nervously or tug it for emphasis.

5. After Harold offers to call the police, leave out all of Harold's daydreaming and continue with Figgy's asking what Harold is going to tell the police.

6. After Figgy tells them that everyone calls his grandfather the Goat Man, continue his speech with his quickly asking whether they have read about his grandfather in the newspaper.

7. Omit the description and continue as Harold clears his throat and tells Figgy to listen.

8. After Harold tells Figgy that his grandfather has locked himself in his old house, leave out the imagining of Harold that he's a news reporter. Continue as surprised Figgy asks Harold what he said.

9. End the scene as Harold says he had better let his mom know they are leaving.

NARRATOR'S CLOSING LINES:

An accident spoils the children's plans, but through it Harold is helped, as are Figgy and his grandfather.

THE ANIMAL, THE VEGETABLE, AND JOHN D. JONES

Betsy Byars

This scene is from an early chapter in which Clara and Deanie have been left alone in the beach house while their father has gone to the airport to pick up Delores and John D. The two sisters are arguing and shouting.

SUGGESTED STAGING:

The narrator stands at a lectern. Clara and Deanie sit on stools.

              Clara   Deanie
                X   X

    Narrator
        X

NARRATOR'S OPENING LINES:

We are presenting a scene from *The Animal, the Vegetable, and John D. Jones* by Betsy Byars. The characters in this scene are two quarreling sisters: Clara, read by _____, and Deanie, read by _____. I, _____, am the narrator.

Clara and Deanie are beginning the first day of their two-week vacation at the beach. They are not, however, happy with the thought of the days ahead. Their divorced dad has invited a friend, Delores, and her son, John D. Jones, to join them for the entire vacation. While their dad is picking up the unwanted guests at the airport, Clara and Deanie are alone in the beach house. Deanie, hoping to be selected cheerleader, is practicing cheers. Clara is sitting in a chair, scrutinizing her legs.

SCRIPTING SUGGESTIONS:

1. Begin as Clara yells, "Fleas!"

2. Instruct Deanie's reader to put a lot of enthusiasm into the cheers and to howl the word "wolves."

3. Instruct Clara's reader to pretend to hold a flea and then to pretend to toss it.

4. After the two shout, "Nyaah," at each other, insert the following lines for the narrator: The two stick out their tongues at each other, happy to suffer insult for the pleasure of speaking their minds. Then Deanie, looking stunned, sits up straight and smiles half-heartedly toward the door.

5. Continue as Clara asks what is wrong.

6. End the scene with Clara's comment about Delores and her cretin son.

NARRATOR'S CLOSING LINES:

And then Deanie sees that indeed Delores and her son *are* standing in the doorway. The father, being the last to enter the room, misses the insults and begins the introductions. John D. comments, "They are just as I imagined." Thus, the vacation that had a bumpy beginning now tilts toward disaster.

THE BLOSSOMS MEET THE VULTURE LADY

Betsy Byars

This scene is taken from chapter 5, "Mad Mary," in which Pap explains Mad Mary's earlier years.

SUGGESTED STAGING:
The narrator stands at a lectern. Pap, Vern, and Maggie sit on chairs.

	Maggie	Vern	Pap
	X	X	X
Narrator			
X			

NARRATOR'S OPENING LINES:
This readers theatre presentation is from *The Blossoms Meet the Vulture Lady* by Betsy Byars. The characters in this scene are three members of the poverty-stricken Blossom family: Maggie, the older sister, read by _____; Vern, the younger brother, read by _____; and the grandfather, Pap, read by _____. I, _____, am the narrator.

On this particular afternoon Pap, Vern, and Maggie are in the pickup truck. They are traveling around picnic areas and searching through trash bins to find aluminum cans. Maggie, having won a seat by the window, is the first to see mad Mary, the vulture lady, standing near the road. Mad Mary takes something from the road and stuffs it into her bag.

SCRIPTING SUGGESTIONS:
1. Begin as Maggie shouts that Mad Mary is there. Instruct the reader to communicate Maggie's excitement.

2. Skip the comments that other kids make about Mary's cane. Continue as Vern asks what she has put in the bag.

3. After Vern asks whether Pap went to school with Mad Mary, instruct Pap's reader to nod his head and say, "yes."

4. At this point insert thc following lines for the narrator: Pap drives the pickup into the park area. The three Blossoms get out, and Pap begins rummaging through the trash cans.

5. Continue by having Vern's reader ask what Mad Mary was like.

6. Omit the description of Pap's search through the waste bins as well as his comments about the various items of trash.

7. As Pap speaks to Mad Mary, instruct the reader to touch his forehead as if to tip a hat.

8. Omit the remaining description, and end the scene with Pap's comments about Mary's shack and about their leaving.

NARRATOR'S CLOSING LINES:
Pap tosses the bags of trash into the back of the pickup, and the Blossoms drive away. Little do they suspect that someone in the "not-just-anybody" family will become Mad Mary's prisoner and dine on varmint stew.

THE BURNING QUESTIONS OF BINGO BROWN

Betsy Byars

This script is taken from two chapters, "The Boy Behind the Rebel Leader" and "Two Setbacks in the T-shirt War."

SUGGESTED STAGING:

The narrator stands at a lectern. Bingo and his mother sit on chairs.

Bingo   Mother

X   X

Narrator

X

NARRATOR'S OPENING LINES:

This script is taken from two separate scenes of the novel *The Burning Questions of Bingo Brown* by Betsy Byars. The two characters in each scene are the human magnet for trouble, Bingo Brown, read by _____, and his mother, read by _____. I, _____, am the narrator.

Bingo and his mother are eating supper when the first surprising conversation takes place. Here Bingo and his mother talk at length and yet communicate very little because Bingo does not realize that his mother is teasing.

SCRIPTING SUGGESTIONS:

1. Begin the script at the point where Bingo asks his mother to guess what has happened.

2. Omit description and movement.

3. Provide instructions so that readers can communicate Bingo's exaggeration and attempts to cover up his mistakes, and his mother's interest, curiosity and tongue-in-cheek humor.

4. After Bingo asks his mother whether she is serious about a wear-in, insert the following lines for the narrator:

   > That question remains unanswered. Bingo's dad returns to the supper table, and the discussion of vulgar T-shirts is suspended until after school the next day when Bingo runs all the way home to tell his mother something that he thinks will make her *proud*. He bursts into the kitchen.

5. Skip the rest of that chapter and the following chapter. Begin again in "Two Setbacks in the T-shirt War" at the point where Bingo shouts to his mother that the wear-in worked.

6. Provide instructions so that the readers can communicate Bingo's excitement and growing uncertainty and his mother's confusion and disbelief.

7. After his mother attempts to threaten him for lying, write the following instructions for Bingo's reader: (He shakes his head no, makes an X on his chest, and then wipes sweat from his brow.)

8. End the scene with the previous motions.

NARRATOR'S CLOSING LINES:

Avoiding a larger confrontation with his mother is only one of Bingo's problems. He must also figure out how to participate in mixed-sex conversations, how to deal with a teacher who is emotionally unstable, and how to avoid violence at the hands of Billy Wentworth; and—more immediately— he must decide what his T-shirt will say on Friday.

CRACKER JACKSON

Betsy Byars

This suggested script is taken from the chapter "Wrong Worries, Right Worries" in which Cracker goes to see Alma.

SUGGESTED STAGING:
The narrator stands at a lectern. Alma is sitting on a chair and Cracker is sitting on a stool.

Alma
X

Cracker
X

Narrator
X

NARRATOR'S OPENING LINES:
The scene we shall read is from *Cracker Jackson* by Betsy Byars. The characters in the scene are Alma, Cracker's ex-babysitter and Nicole's mother, read by _____, and worried eleven-year-old Cracker, read by _____. I, _____, am the narrator.

Cracker sees Alma at McDonald's and she has a black eye. He is sure Billy Ray, her husband, is beating her. Today, Cracker receives an unsigned note that says, "Keep away, Cracker, or he'll hurt you." He is sure the note is from Alma. Afraid for her, Cracker goes to Alma's house that evening to see if she is all right. Fortunately, Billy Ray's truck is not in the driveway and Alma is sitting on the porch with her baby, Nicole.

SCRIPTING SUGGESTIONS:
1. Begin the scene by having Cracker say, "Hi," to Alma.

2. Omit Alma's line to Nicole. Combine Alma's answer that Cracker just did not notice with her lines assuring Cracker that Billy Ray did not beat up on her.

3. After Alma asks Cracker to promise not to tell his mother, omit the memories Cracker has of Alma's desire to be slim. Continue with Cracker's statement to Alma that he got her letter.

4. Be sure Alma's reader has directions that show Alma's fright when she sees her husband's pickup.

5. End the scene as Alma tells Cracker not to let Billy Ray see him.

NARRATOR'S CLOSING LINES:
Cracker gets away without being seen, but in the weeks that follow, he has many reasons to fear Billy Ray before Alma's life becomes better.

THE CYBIL WAR

Betsy Byars

This recommended scene is from the chapter, "Popsicle Legs and Tub of Blubber" in which Tony delivers his first insults.

SUGGESTED STAGING:

                                          Tony
                                           X
                    Simon   Harriett
                      X   X

        Narrator
           X

NARRATOR'S OPENING LINES:

We are reading a scene from *The Cybil War* by Betsy Byars. The characters are Simon, who is the main character, read by _____; Tony, his not-so-truthful friend, read by _____; and their classmate Harriet, read by _____. I, _____, am the narrator.

Simon's class is involved in producing a play about nutrition. Neither Simon nor Tony is pleased with his part. Tony is playing a pickle. Cybil Ackerman, whom Simon loves, has wrangled the role of indigestion, and Simon is left with the part of peanut butter. Harriet comes by to find out if Simon is angry with Cybil because she has won the role of indigestion. As she walks up, Tony is doing a perfect imitation of his little sister.

SCRIPTING SUGGESTIONS:

1. Begin with Tony's imitation.

2. Have Harriet address Simon by his name when she asks whether he is angry.

3. At the appropriate time, instruct Harriet's reader to gasp.

4. After Tony asks Harriet to wait, insert the following lines for the narrator: Tony's last string of remarks are said to Harriet's back. Her whole body trembles with anger as she turns, marches down the hall, and goes into the restroom.

5. Omit movement and description.

6. Although Tony calls Harriet by her last name, use only her first in the script.

7. After Tony notes that Harriet has not forgiven Simon, insert the following lines for the narrator: Harriet storms out of the restroom and retraces her steps. This time she is not alone; two friends advance up the hall with her.

8. Continue with Tony's insults.

9. End the script at the end of the chapter.

NARRATOR'S CLOSING LINES:

Tony may be just getting started in telling lies, but it is Simon who remains the subject of those lies. Simon's love for Cybil Ackerman motivates Tony to even more outrageous falsehoods and insults, and the war that breaks out is nothing less than *The Cybil War*.

THE HOUSE OF WINGS

Betsy Byars

This suggested script is adapted from the chapter "GIT!" in which Sammy's grandfather discovers the wounded crane.

SUGGESTED STAGING:

The narrator stands at a lectern. Sammy and his grandfather sit on stools.

Sammy   Grandfather

X   X

Narrator

X

NARRATOR'S OPENING LINES:

The scene that we have chosen to share is from *The House of Wings* by Betsy Byars. The characters in this scene are Sammy, an angry boy, read by _____, and his nature-loving grandfather, read by _____. I, _____, am the narrator.

Sammy and his parents are driving to Detroit where the father hopes to find work. They stop in Ohio to stay overnight with a grandfather Sammy does not remember. While Sammy is asleep, his parents leave him there. Sammy is so angry when his grandfather tries to explain that he begins to run. His grandfather chases him, but suddenly he calls to Sammy. Afraid the grandfather is hurt, Sammy goes back. His grandfather tells him to look as he points to a bird, over three feet tall, with long legs like stilts.

SCRIPTING SUGGESTIONS:

1. Begin the scene as Sammy asks his grandfather what it is and his grandfather answers that it is a crane.

2. Be sure to include directions for Sammy's reader to show such emotions as anger and scorn in his voice, as the narration suggests.

3. After Sammy starts to repeat that no crane he knew ever got to be twenty-one, let the narrator interrupt to say: While Sammy is speaking, Sammy's grandfather moves a step forward and the nervous crane runs his wing feathers between his beak again and again.

4. Continue with Sammy's lines that ask why the crane is making that motion.

5. Do not have the characters leave their seats even though the dialogue indicates they inch closer to the crane.

6. End the scene as Sammy says he wishes the crane would just fall down dead.

NARRATOR'S CLOSING LINES:

Sammy throws a rock at the crane. His angry grandfather tells him to run to Detroit, and no one will follow him. But as his furious grandfather yells "Sit," Sammy feels compelled to stay. Because they rescue the wounded crane and care for it in his grandfather's dilapidated old house, Sammy's anger disappears and he begins to care.

THE MIDNIGHT FOX

Betsy Byars

This scene is from chapter 1, "Bad News," in which Tommy learns that he must spend the summer with Aunt Millie.

SUGGESTED STAGING:

The narrator stands at a lectern. Tommy, his mother, and his father sit on chairs.

	Tommy	Mother	
	X	X	
			Father
			X
Narrator			
X			

NARRATOR'S OPENING LINES:

We are presenting a scene from *The Midnight Fox* by Betsy Byars. The characters in this scene are ten-year-old Tommy, read by _____; his mother, read by _____; and his father, read by _____. I, _____, am the narrator.

Tommy's parents are schoolteachers, and this summer they have the opportunity to take a bicycle tour of five European countries. His mother wants Tommy to spend the summer with Aunt Millie, and in an excited way she explains that he will be able to spend two months on his aunt and uncle's farm. As she is talking, Tommy is unwrapping a new model airplane, and the news makes him feel terrible.

SCRIPTING SUGGESTIONS:

1. Begin with Tommy's statement that he does not want to go.

2. Omit movement and description.

3. After Tommy says that strange animals charge him all the time, include the following lines for the narrator: His mother continues explaining the joys of country living until she realizes that Tommy is daydreaming and not listening. Then she changes the focus of her argument.

4. Continue with the mother's next line.

5. Omit the paragraph that explains that Tommy's mother and father are athletic.

6. Add to Tommy's lines about Mrs. Albergotti the explanation that she has been his babysitter.

7. After his mother says that his father will talk to him, insert the following lines for the narrator:

   His mother leaves the room, and Tommy hears her crying from her room across the hall. Tommy is working on his model airplane later that evening when his father enters his room. Tommy knows that his father will be less understanding than his mother has been.

8. Continue with his father's line about opportunity.

9. Instruct Tommy's reader that Tommy is almost crying when he says he *wants* to go to the farm and that he is sarcastic when he says he wants a pig.

10. End the scene with Tommy's statement that his father can tell his mother that he will go to the farm. At that point instruct Tommy's reader to wipe his eyes and nose.

NARRATOR'S CLOSING LINES:

Tommy's father leaves, and Tommy half-heartedly continues working on his Cessna 180 model. The last thing that Tommy expects is that his outrage will be transformed into joy by the pure magic of a black fox that runs through the meadows as free as the wind, or that in the crashing thunderstorm of a summer night he will find unsuspected and unselfish reserves of courage.

THE SUMMER OF THE SWANS

Betsy Byars

This scene is taken from the chapter that contains Sara and Wanda's conversation after the lights are out at night. They have been to see the swans, but Charlie is not yet missing.

SUGGESTED STAGING:

The narrator stands at a lectern. Sara, Wanda, and Aunt Willie sit on stools.

Sara   Wanda
X   X

Aunt Willie
X

Narrator
X

NARRATOR'S OPENING LINES:

Our readers theatre presentation is from *The Summer of the Swans* by Betsy Byars. The characters in this scene are fourteen-year-old Sara, read by _____; her older sister Wanda, read by _____; and the aunt with whom they live, Aunt Willie, read by _____. I, _____, am the narrator.

This summer is different from all of Sara's other summers. This summer Sara is filled with discontent. She pities Charlie, her younger retarded brother; she envies Wanda; she finds fault with Aunt Willie; and she is unhappy with herself.

On this particular night she has taken Charlie to see the swans, and Wanda has been out with Frank, her boyfriend. Sara, Aunt Willie, and Charlie are in bed in their own rooms, and the lights are out when Wanda comes home. In the dark Wanda stumbles over furniture in the bedroom that she shares with Sara.

SCRIPTING SUGGESTIONS:

1. Begin as Sara tells Wanda that she may turn on the light.

2. Omit movement and action.

3. Provide instructions so that Sara's reader can communicate her frustration and boredom.

4. End the scene with Sara's asking Wanda whether she is really asleep.

NARRATOR'S CLOSING LINES:

A nearly silent presence in the house is Charlie. As the other three finally drop off to sleep, Charlie's foot taps rhythmically and softly against the wall. However, unlike other nights the tapping ceases, and Charlie's actions shock Sara out of her own self-centered miseries.

TROUBLE RIVER

Betsy Byars

This suggested script is taken from chapter 1 where Grandma finds out about the raft.

SUGGESTED STAGING:

The narrator stands at a lectern. Grandma sits in a rocking chair and Dewey sits on the floor.

Grandma   Dewey

X   X

Narrator

X

NARRATOR'S OPENING LINES:

The scene we shall read is from *Trouble River* by Betsy Byars. The characters are Grandma, read by _____, who is fearful of the prairie and being left alone in a cabin with her grandson Dewey, read by _____. I, _____, am the narrator.

Pa has taken Dewey's mother to Hunter City to have her baby. Dewey feels sure his cautious father would not have left them alone if there were anything to fear. Dewey has been down at the river and Grandma has an uneasy feeling.

SCRIPTING SUGGESTIONS:

1. Begin the scene as Grandma sits in her rocking chair and asks Dewey again what he was doing at the river.

2. Be sure to give Grandma's reader directions (firmly, disgustedly, stubbornly, etc.).

3. After Dewey tells Grandma that somebody has to look after the animals, end the scene as Grandma tells Dewey to bar the door.

NARRATOR'S CLOSING LINES:

Grandma's uneasy feeling proves right, and Dewey's raft becomes their only means of escape.

Part IV
SUGGESTED SCRIPTS

THE JOURNEY OF THE SHADOW BAIRNS

Margaret J. Anderson

This suggested script is taken from chapter 1 in which Papa announces to the family that they are going to Canada.

SUGGESTED STAGING:
The narrator stands at a lectern. Papa, Mama, Robbie, and Elspeth are seated in chairs.

	Mama	Papa	
	X	X	
Elspeth			Robbie
X			X

Narrator
X

NARRATOR'S OPENING LINES:
The scene that we have chosen to share is from *The Journey of the Shadow Bairns* by Margaret Anderson. The characters in this scene are Papa, a shipyard worker, read by _____; Mama, his sickly wife, read by _____; thirteen-year-old Elspeth, who misses the farm on which they used to live, read by _____; and four-year-old Robbie, who has lived his life in a one-room tenement, read by _____. I, _____, am the narrator.

It is November 1902, and Papa has come home early from the Glasgow, Scotland shipyards. He assures his family that he brings good news as well as hot pies from the bakery. However, it isn't until after supper that he pulls a pamphlet from his pocket and shares his excitement.

SCRIPTING SUGGESTIONS:
1. Begin the scene when Papa asks Mama if she would like to go to Canada.

2. Instruct Mama's reader to let her become more interested and appear happier, humming a song, etc. as the scene progresses.

3. End the scene by having Elspeth read the paragraph from the pamphlet about the land of the brave.

NARRATOR'S CLOSING LINES:
The pamphlet promises much, but tragedy strikes and Elspeth and Robbie have to set out for Canada alone. The perils are many, but after a year and a half, Elspeth is able to look to the future with hope and happiness.

GRAY BOY

Jim Arnosky

This suggested script is taken from chapter 2 where Uncle Bill stops to see Ian and his mother.

SUGGESTED STAGING:
The narrator stands at a lectern. Uncle Bill, Ian, and his mother sit on chairs.

Lucy   Uncle Bill
X   X

Ian
X

Narrator
X

NARRATOR'S OPENING LINES:
The scene we have chosen to share is from *Gray Boy* by Jim Arnosky. The characters in this scene are Lucy, a young widow who works in the school cafeteria, read by _____; her thirteen-year-old son Ian, read by _____; and Uncle Bill, Lucy's brother, read by _____. I, _____, am the narrator.

As the scene opens, Gray Boy, the dog given to Ian by his father just before he died, has not returned home for supper. Ian sees his Uncle Bill's truck drive up and figures his uncle has found the dog wandering along the roadside and has brought him home. However, Uncle Bill has stopped to visit with Lucy and Ian about two hunting beagles he has just purchased.

SCRIPTING SUGGESTIONS:
1. Begin the scene with Uncle Bill's speech about picking up the new dogs in Warren. However, have him say he is going to pick up the two beagles in Warren in order to make his speech clear to the audience.

2. Give the readers instructions, such as worried, confidently, seriously, etc., as the speeches continue.

3. When Ian tells Uncle Bill that he'll get the leather collars, have him get up and walk out because he is not in the scene again on stage.

4. Let Uncle Bill speak as soon as Ian is gone.

5. End the scene by having Ian shout from offstage that he wants Uncle Bill and his mother to come help him with Gray Boy.

NARRATOR'S CLOSING LINES:
Before Uncle Bill and Ian's mother can move, however, there is a pounding at the front door. Is it already too late to make a decision about Gray Boy?

MR. POPPER'S PENGUINS

Richard and Florence Atwater

This suggested script is taken from chapter 2 in which the radio voice promises Mr. Popper a surprise.

SUGGESTED STAGING:

The narrator stands at a lectern. Mr. and Mrs. Popper are seated in chairs.

Mr. Popper   Mrs. Popper

X   X

Narrator

X

NARRATOR'S OPENING LINES:

The characters for this scene from *Mr. Popper's Penguins* by Richard and Florence Atwater are Mr. Popper, a house painter, read by _____; and Mrs. Popper, his patient wife, read by _____. I, _____, am the narrator. _____ is the radio voice offstage.

It is evening in the Popper house on September 29 and Mr. Popper will be out of work until spring. Since he is fascinated by polar explorers, he is contented because he can spend the whole winter reading travel books about Antarctica. Mrs. Popper is worried about whether the food money will last.

SCRIPTING SUGGESTIONS:

1. Mrs. Popper is mending clothes, and Mr. Popper is reading as the scene opens.

2. In the opening speech Mrs. Popper asks Mr. Popper what he is reading.

3. Have Mrs. Popper yawn but not move as she says she is going to bed.

4. Have the radio on a chair or small table near Mr. Popper so he does not need to move to turn it on.

5. The radio does not need to buzz. The voice need not be faint.

6. Mr. Popper does not need to locate the Antarctic on the globe before he asks his wife what she supposes the surprise is.

7. End the scene by having Mrs. Popper say that she does not want to be late to the Ladies' Aid meeting.

NARRATOR'S CLOSING LINES:

Even Mr. Popper is not prepared for the surprise. The next day an expressman delivers the largest box Mr. Popper has ever seen. It is covered with markings that say "Keep Cool." A faint "ork" sound is the beginning of an adventure that ends when Mr. Popper realizes his dream.

TUCK EVERLASTING

Natalie Babbitt

This scene is from chapter 7, which contains the Tucks' explanation of the spring's mysterious power.

SUGGESTED STAGING:
The narrator stands at a lectern. Ma Tuck, Winnie, Jesse, and Miles sit on stools.

Winnie   Jesse

X   X

Ma Tuck   Miles

X   X

Narrator

X

NARRATOR'S OPENING LINES:
This readers theatre presentation is from *Tuck Everlasting* by Natalie Babbitt. The characters are the wise and loving Ma Tuck, read by _____; Winnie Foster, a ten-year-old girl, read by _____; and Ma Tuck's two sons, Jesse, read by _____, and Miles, read by _____. I, _____, am the narrator.

This scene begins after the Tucks have kidnapped Winnie Foster just as she attempts to drink from a spring in the woods. They have ended a speedy and bouncy horseback ride by stopping among bushes just off the road. The three Tucks are eager to explain that they are friends who want to keep Winnie only long enough to tell her about their strange experiences with the spring in the woods. It is the most remarkable story that Winnie has ever heard.

SCRIPTING SUGGESTIONS:
1. Begin the scene with the narrative passage that explains how the Tucks found the spring eighty-seven years ago.

2. The first lines to be adapted into the scripts, as well as several others that follow, are descriptive passages that will need to be changed into dialogue and assigned to one of the Tucks. Therefore, at the beginning, have Miles say: "Eighty-seven years ago we left the East and came to this part of the country. We were looking for a place to settle. One night we set up a camp near the spring, which was at that time surrounded by a huge forest."

3. Follow those lines with Jesse's comment about the forest being nice.

4. Give Jesse's reader instructions to sigh when he delivers his comment about the nice forest.

5. Adapt and add to Miles's lines about their putting up a house for Ma the explanation that the Tucks had traveled out of the forest and had settled on a farm in a valley. Change "they" to "we."

6. Rewrite the paragraph about the passage of time, revealing that none of the Tucks grew any older, so that it can be read by Jesse, and then assign it to him. Give the reader instructions to be very serious when reading those lines. Again, change "they" to "we."

7. Also, rewrite the paragraph about their remembering that the cat had lived a normal life so that it can be read by Jesse; assign it to him. Again, change "they" to "we."

8. End the scene where the chapter ends.

NARRATOR'S CLOSING LINES:
Winnie can barely believe what she has heard, but she knows what the Tucks told her is true. She also knows that, although she has no choice but to go with them, they will not hurt her. The Tucks reveal even more secrets that throw Winnie into a dangerous adventure and force her to make difficult decisions that affect not only her future but also that of the Tucks.

WHO KNEW THERE'D BE GHOSTS?

Bill Brittain

This script is from chapter 1, "Fancy Shoes and Black Boots," in which Tommy, Books, and Harry the Blimp have their first glimpse of the villains.

SUGGESTED STAGING:
The narrator stands at a lectern. Tommy, Books, and Harry the Blimp sit on stools.

		Books	
	Tommy	X	Harry the Blimp
Narrator	X		X
X			

NARRATOR'S OPENING LINES:
We are sharing a scene from *Who Knew There'd Be Ghosts?* by Bill Brittain. The characters are three seventh-graders: Tommy, the unpredictable schemer, read by _____; Books, the class brain, read by _____; and Harry the Blimp, read by _____. I, _____, am the narrator.

One day, while Tommy, Books, and Harry the Blimp are playing at the old Parnell House, two strangers drive up and then walk around the yard. Hiding under a spruce tree, the three friends can identify the two only by their shoes: Black Boots and Fancy Shoes. Clearly the two intruders are up to no good.

SCRIPTING SUGGESTIONS:

1. Begin the script with Books's statement that the two have gone.

2. At the appropriate time, instruct Harry's and Tommy's readers simultaneously to shake their heads and to say, "No."

3. In order for the audience to understand Tommy's attitude about playing in the park, write his lines so that those thoughts are spoken.

4. Instead of Tommy's thinking about spending the night inside Parnell House, rewrite his lines so that they may be read.

5. At the point where it appears that Tommy is the only one who can spend the first night inside Parnell House, instruct both Harry the Blimp and Books to look at him.

6. End the scene after Harry mentions the games.

NARRATOR'S CLOSING LINES:
A few minutes later Tommy is plodding home. He is preparing himself to wait alone in Parnell House for the return of Black Boots, but WHO KNEW THERE'D BE GHOSTS?

THE WISH GIVER

Bill Brittain

This suggested scene is from the prologue, "The Strange Little Man," where Thaddeus Blinn promises each of four characters (Stew Meat, Polly, Rowena, and Adam) the fulfillment of a single wish.

SUGGESTED STAGING:

The narrator stands at a lectern. Thaddeus sits on a stool. Polly, Rowena, Adam, and Stew Meat sit in chairs.

	Adam		Polly	
	X		X	Thaddeus Blinn
Stew Meat		Rowena		X
X		X		
Narrator				
X				

NARRATOR'S OPENING LINES:

We shall share the opening scene from Bill Brittain's fantasy *The Wish Giver*. The characters are an odd, self-proclaimed wish fulfiller, Thaddeus Blinn, read by _____; outspoken Polly Kemp, read by _____; a farm boy, Adam Fiske, read by _____; love-stricken Rowena, read by _____; and Stew Meat, the general store proprietor, read by _____. I, _____, am the narrator.

While attending the Coven Tree Church social, Thaddeus Blinn has drawn Polly, Adam, Rowena, and Stew Meat into a ragged tent. Thaddeus promises for fifty cents to sell each the fulfillment of a single wish. Polly is unpopular with her peers; Adam is tired of hauling water for his father's farm; and Rowena is in love with a traveling salesman.

SCRIPTING SUGGESTIONS:

1. Although Stew Meat is the narrator in the novel, in the script he should share the same point of view as the other characters. Therefore, some narration must be rewritten so that it can be read as though it were spoken by that character.

2. Begin the script with Adam's complaint that he has been in the tent for nearly half an hour.

3. Provide instructions to help the readers interpret the feeling of the lines. The first such instruction should be to read Adam's first lines impatiently. Other instructions can be developed from the text's vivid words (e.g., "peevishly," "singsong," and "piped up").

4. Include some instruction for small motions, such as having Blinn "spread his hands" to indicate that selling wishes is the "most obvious thing in the world."

5. For the section that explains their buying the wishes, include the following narrator's speech: At that point Stew Meat, Polly, Rowena, and Adam slowly reach into their pockets and wallets, and then each hands Thaddeus Blinn fifty cents. He puts the change into his pocket and gives each of them a single white card. There is a red spot on each card.

6. Omit two paragraphs: the one that begins with the words, "Polly glared," and the other with the words, "I guess all four."

NARRATOR'S CLOSING LINES:

Did the four characters believe Thaddeus Blinn? Stew Meat considers the possibility and then slips his card into his store's cash register drawer. Polly, Adam, and Rowena keep their cards and make wishes for what they want most. Those three get exactly what they wish for—well, *nearly* exactly what they wish for.

SHOESHINE GIRL

Clyde Robert Bulla

The following suggested scene is from chapter 1, "Palmville," in which Aunt Claudia meets Sara Ida's train and takes Sara Ida home with her.

SUGGESTED STAGING:

The narrator stands at a lectern. Sara Ida and Aunt Claudia sit on stools.

Sara Ida   Aunt Claudia

X   X

Narrator

X

NARRATOR'S OPENING LINES:

This readers theatre presentation is taken from the opening chapter of *Shoeshine Girl* by Clyde Robert Bulla. The characters in this scene are rebellious Sara Ida, read by _____, and patient but firm Aunt Claudia, read by _____. I, _____, am the narrator.

Because Sara Ida has been involved in a shoplifting incident, her parents send her to spend the summer with Aunt Claudia. Aunt Claudia meets her at the train, and she is now helping Sara Ida move into her room.

SCRIPTING SUGGESTIONS:

1. Begin the scene as Aunt Claudia shows Sara Ida the telephone.

2. Include instructions so that the two readers are able to interpret Aunt Claudia's warm, but matter-of-fact approach and Sara Ida's hostile and resentful attitude.

3. Omit all references to moving from one area of the house to another; however, include some small motions (e.g., Aunt Claudia's opening and closing her mouth as though she changes her mind about what to say).

4. Skip the section that begins when Aunt Claudia asks Sara Ida to come upstairs and that ends with the description of the pictures on the wall.

5. Have the two characters read the lines that Sara Ida imagines as though they are spoken.

6. Change Aunt Claudia's question, "How do you like it?" to "How do you like your room?"

7. End the scene with Aunt Claudia's suggestion that Sara Ida rest.

NARRATOR'S CLOSING LINES:

Sara Ida wants to cry, but she knows that crying will accomplish nothing. Too unhappy to do anything else, she gets up and unpacks her suitcase. Little does she know that by the summer's end she will become a shoeshine girl ready to make sacrifices for her friends and family.

IDA EARLY COMES OVER THE MOUNTAIN

Robert Burch

This suggested script is taken from the "Bedding Down" chapter when Ida spends her first evening with the Sutton family.

SUGGESTED STAGING:

The narrator stands at a lectern. The other characters are seated on chairs.

                                        Aunt Earnestine
                          Mr. Sutton   X   Ida
                Randall   X   X   Clay
        Ellen   X   X   Dewey
Narrator X   X
   X

NARRATOR'S OPENING LINES:

In the scene we are sharing from Robert Burch's *Ida Early Comes Over the Mountain,* the characters are Ida, a job-hunting, scarecrowlike woman, read by _____; bossy Aunt Earnestine, who is the current family caretaker, read by _____; Mr. Sutton, a hard-working widower, read by _____; Ellen, a pretty twelve-year-old, read by _____; Randall, Ellen's eleven-year-old brother, read by _____; and the five-year-old twins Clay and Dewey, read by _____ and _____. I, _____, am the narrator.

Ida Early is wearing overalls and clodhopper shoes as she knocks on the door of the Sutton house and asks for work. Ida is hired because Aunt Earnestine, who has cared for the family since Mrs. Sutton's death, wants to go back to Atlanta. While Aunt Earnestine and Mr. Sutton are in town, Ida plays with the children, and Randall and Ellen cook the stew. That evening at supper, Mr. Randall praises the meal.

SCRIPTING SUGGESTIONS:

1. Begin the scene by having Mr. Sutton say that it is too bad they cannot invite a king to the meal.

2. After Ida pretends to powder her face and fluff her hair, let everyone laugh, including Ida, as she tells Clay that he has never seen her when she is fixed up.

3. Then let the narrator say: After supper Mr. Sutton unfolds the newspaper and hands the comic strip section to the twins.

4. Let Clay call Ellen by name as he asks her to read the funnies.

5. It is not necessary for Aunt Earnestine to go to her room or for the twins and Ida to move their chairs.

6. Let Clay say, "So do we!" but omit the lines asking her to read some more.

7. After Ida says she has never known dirty dishes to run away, let the narrator read the following lines: Ida reads to the twins while Ellen and Randall do the dishes. They don't mind and enjoy listening to Ida read. Aunt Earnestine is so angry she looks as if she could explode. Then Ida puts the twins to bed, singing and yodeling a lullaby before returning to the kitchen.

8. After the narrator's previous lines, continue as Aunt Earnestine tells Ida she can go home.

9. After Ida tells them she slept in the barn feed room last night, let Aunt Earnestine say in a shocked tone, "You can't sleep in the barn. It isn't proper."

10. Add a speech for Mr. Sutton in which he hesitantly says, "I guess it will be all right for you to sleep in one of the feed rooms, Ida. But I insist you take from the house a blanket and a quilt."

11. Ida need not go to the door as she asks them to wake her when breakfast is ready.

12. End the scene with Ida's lines about thoughtfulness.

NARRATOR'S CLOSING LINES:

Ida makes life enjoyable for the children with her tall tales and loving ways. However, Ellen and Randall must learn the responsibility of true friendship before the family can be truly happy.

THE ENORMOUS EGG

Oliver Butterworth

This suggested script is taken from chapter 3 in which Nate meets Dr. Zeimer.

SUGGESTED STAGING:

The narrator stands at a lectern. Nate and Dr. Zeimer sit on chairs.

	Nate	Dr. Zeimer
	X	X
Narrator		
X		

NARRATOR'S OPENING LINES:

The characters in our scene from *The Enormous Egg* by Oliver Butterworth are Nate Twitchell, the caretaker of the family's chickens, read by _____, and a paleozoologist, Dr. Zeimer, read by _____. I, _____, am the narrator.

After Nate Twitchell discovers one of their hens sitting on an enormous egg with a leathery shell, Nate's father, a newspaperman, decides Nate can let the hen sit on it to see if it will hatch. His father writes a story about it for the newspaper. A month goes by, but the egg does not hatch. A discouraged Nate goes fishing and a stranger rows near Nate's boat.

SCRIPTING SUGGESTIONS:

1. Begin the scene by having the stranger ask Nate if he is having any luck.

2. Do not have Nate pause after the stranger asks him if he lives around there. Let Nate nod and continue his speech that he lives in town.

3. After the stranger offers his sandwich and says he does not need it, create a speech for Nate instead of using a narrator. Let Nate say: "No, thank you. I have to go home to lunch anyway."

4. After Dr. Zeimer offers his sandwich again because he cannot stand to have a hungry boy watching him, let Nate say: "Thank you. I am hungry."

5. Let Dr. Zeimer pause *very* briefly before he comments about the leathery shell. As soon as Nate nods, continue with Dr. Zeimer's next speech.

6. End the scene by having Nate agree to take Dr. Zeimer to look at the egg.

NARRATOR'S CLOSING LINES:

Dr. Zeimer sees the egg and predicts that it may hatch in a week. He urges that they protect it, as the newborn may have an unusual appearance when it hatches. His prediction proves true, and in the months that follow, Nate enlists the assistance of the whole country in order to save his pet.

ELLEN TEBBITS

Beverly Cleary

This suggested script is taken from chapter 1 where Ellen discovers that Austine also must wear old-fashioned woolen underwear in winter.

SUGGESTED STAGING:

The narrator stands at a lectern. Ellen and Austine are seated on stools. Barbara, Linda and Joanne are seated in chairs.

Ellen   Austine
X   X

Joanne
X

Linda   Barbara
X   X

Narrator
X

NARRATOR'S OPENING LINES:

In the scene we are sharing from *Ellen Tebbits* by Beverly Cleary, the characters are thin, dark-haired Ellen, who has no really best friend, read by _____; Austine, a good-natured, untidy new girl, read by _____; and three other ballet students, Linda, Joanne and Barbara, read by _____, _____, and _____. I, _____, am the narrator.

Ellen is embarrassed because her mother makes her wear old-fashioned woolen underwear, even to ballet class. Ellen hides in the janitor's broom closet, slips her arms out of the hated underwear, rolls the top around her waist, and puts on her costume. However, during class the underwear slips. Otis Spofford imitates her as she tries to keep the underwear from falling further and dance at the same time. Austine quickly accuses Otis of bumping her and he goes away. Ellen is grateful, and after class she tries to slip into the broom closet and dress. To her surprise Austine is already in the broom closet, and she, too, is wearing woolen underwear.

SCRIPTING SUGGESTIONS:

1. Begin the scene by having Austine order Ellen to shut the door.

2. When Linda says, "I'll bet they're in there," add the following to her speech: "I'm going to open the door and find out." Then continue with, "There you are!"

3. After Ellen suggests to Austine that they go home, let the narrator say: As the girls walk home, they begin to get acquainted.

4. End the scene with the close of the chapter.

NARRATOR'S CLOSING LINES:

Ellen and Austine have good times together, but through a misunderstanding, Ellen slaps Austine and the friendship ends. Not until it is time to wear the hated underwear again does Ellen take advantage of an opportunity to say she is sorry.

RAMONA AND HER FATHER

Beverly Cleary

This suggested script is adapted from the first scene in the book, in which Ramona is preparing her Christmas list.

SUGGESTED STAGING:

The narrator stands at a lectern. Beezus and Mrs. Quimby are seated in chairs. Ramona sits behind a small table.

Ramona   Mrs. Quimby

X   X   Beezus

X

Narrator

X

NARRATOR'S OPENING LINES:

In the scene we are sharing from Beverly Cleary's *Ramona and Her Father,* Ramona, a cheerful second-grader, is read by _____; Beezus, her seventh-grade sister, is read by _____; and Mrs. Quimby, their patient mother, is read by _____. I, _____, am the narrator.

It is a late September afternoon and Ramona is preparing a list of gifts she wants for Christmas. Mrs. Quimby, who has just taken a part-time job, is discouraged as she ponders what to have for supper. Beezus has not yet arrived home from school.

SCRIPTING SUGGESTIONS:

1. Begin the scene by having Ramona sing "yeep" twice as she writes.

2. Omit Mrs. Quimby's action of looking in the refrigerator. Her lines do not make action necessary.

3. Let Ramona say, "Leftovers—yuck," instead of thinking it. Complete her speech with her describing soft hamburgers, etc., and saying they *are* her favorite treat. Continue with the line about feeling snug and cozy. End her speech as she says that she and Beezus never quarrel at a Whopperburger.

4. Sighing loudly, Beezus comes in from the side and drops in a chair.

5. End the scene as Mrs. Quimby tells Beezus that she will see what she can do.

NARRATOR'S CLOSING LINES:

The family does not eat out that night. When Father arrives home he has lost his job. In the months that follow, Ramona tries unsuccessfully to make money to contribute to the family income. The girls go on a campaign to make Father quit smoking. By Christmas Ramona realizes that, although there are problems, they *are* a happy family because they love each other.

THE GET-AWAY CAR

Eleanor Clymer

This suggested script is taken from chapter 1 where Aunt Ruby comes to take Maggie away from Grandma.

SUGGESTED STAGING:
The narrator stands at a lectern. Grandma and Maggie are seated in chairs and Aunt Ruby is seated on a stool.

```
                    Grandma        Maggie
                      X              X
                                            Aunt Ruby
                                               X
        Narrator
           X
```

NARRATOR'S OPENING LINES:
The characters in the scene we shall read from *The Get-Away Car* by Eleanor Clymer are fun-loving Grandma, read by _____; her concerned granddaughter Maggie, read by _____; and persistent Aunt Ruby, read by _____. I, _____, am the narrator.

Maggie has lived with her grandma since her parents separated when she was five. Aunt Ruby wants Maggie and stops in often to complain that Maggie doesn't eat properly, the apartment is shabby, and the neighborhood is dangerous. As the scene opens, Grandma and Maggie are arriving home from a picnic with Maggie's friends. Grandma took them in a cab, and Maggie is worried about spending the money. They discuss it as they climb the stairs to their apartment.

SCRIPTING SUGGESTIONS:
1. Begin by having Maggie tell Grandma that it was sneaky of her to take a cab.

2. After Grandma says tuna fish and spaghetti will have to do, let the narrator say: They arrive at the apartment and Grandma reaches for her key. Then she stops and gasps, for she sees a light under the door.

3. After Maggie screams that they may have a gun, let the narrator say: To their surprise, Aunt Ruby opens the door.

4. After Aunt Ruby comments that it is about time they return, continue with her speech asking them where they have been.

5. After Grandma tells Aunt Ruby to stand out of the way, let the narrator say: As Aunt Ruby steps aside, Grandma walks in and sits down with a thump. She closes her eyes.

6. After Maggie tells Aunt Ruby that she does not want to stay with her, omit Maggie's action of going to the kitchen and the first part of Aunt Ruby's next speech. Let her begin with her telling Margaret Agnes to be ready.

7. After Grandma says she is going to lie down, let the narrator say: Grandma shuffles slowly to her bedroom as if she is too tired to talk. Maggie knows Grandma is just putting on an act for Aunt Ruby.

8. End the scene when Aunt Ruby says good-bye to Maggie.

NARRATOR'S CLOSING LINES:
Aunt Ruby slams the door when she leaves, and Maggie kicks it in anger. Unfortunately, Aunt Ruby is determined. In an effort to avoid Aunt Ruby until she goes back to California, Grandma rents an old car and takes Maggie and three of her friends to see Cousin Esther, whom she has not heard from in years. It was an eventful trip in what actually turns out to be a get-away car. Fortunately, it all ends well.

THANK YOU, JACKIE ROBINSON

Barbara Cohen

This script is taken from chapter 1 in which Sam and Davy become acquainted.

SUGGESTED STAGING:

The narrator stands at a lectern. Sam and Davy sit on stools.

Sam   Davy

X   X

Narrator

X

NARRATOR'S OPENING LINES:

Our readers theatre presentation is from *Thank You, Jackie Robinson* by Barbara Cohen. The characters are two Dodgers fans: Sam, a fatherless white boy, read by _____, and a sixty-year-old black cook, Davy, read by _____. I, _____, am the narrator.

The friendship between Davy and Sam begins the afternoon that they meet in the kitchen of Sam's mother's inn. Davy is making apple pies.

SCRIPTING SUGGESTIONS:

1. Begin as Davy says, "Hello."

2. In order to omit description and movement, entire sentences and paragraphs that have no dialogue will be skipped at various points.

3. End the scene with Davy's statement that he has no children except Henrietta.

NARRATOR'S CLOSING LINES:

After that meeting their friendship grows so strong that Sam counts on Davy's friendship for life. They pore over Dodgers articles on the sports pages, listen to Dodgers games on the radio and watch them on T.V., and—to Sam's astonishment—attend Dodgers games. However, nothing stays the same, and Sam learns that more important than the Dodgers is having someone special with whom to share things.

THE HOUSE OF SIXTY FATHERS

Meindert DeJong

This suggested readers theatre presentation is taken from chapter 1, "Rain on the Sampan," from the point when Tien Pao returns the sampan to where his mother and father are waiting for him.

SUGGESTED STAGING:
The narrator stands at a lectern. Tien Pao, his mother, and his father sit on stools.

Tien Pao
X

Mother   Father
X   X

Narrator
X

NARRATOR'S OPENING LINES:
This scene is from *The House of Sixty Fathers* by Meindert DeJong. The characters are Tien Pao, a small Chinese boy, read by _____; his frightened mother, read by _____; and his father, read by _____. I, _____, am the narrator.

By traveling up a river in their sampan, Tien Pao and his family have escaped from a Japanese attack on the coast of China. Now refugees, the family is living on the sampan wedged in the mud of the riverbank. Tien Pao's mother and father work during the day, and Tien Pao's responsibility is to stay on the sampan and never to take it from the bank. When an American airman offers him one hundred yen for a ferry ride across the river, Tien Pao decides his father would approve, and he takes the soldier across and back. On his return the sampan slams into the mud of the riverbank, and, because the trip has taken much longer than he expected, Tien Pao is met by his worried, rain-drenched, exhausted, and hungry mother and father.

SCRIPTING SUGGESTIONS:
1. Begin the scene with the mother calling out to Tien Pao. Instruct the reader to communicate misery and fear in the mother's voice. Have her call out to Tien Pao two or three times before he answers.

2. This scene will require the omission of much description, and the emotion that is described should be communicated through the voices of the readers. Therefore, provide adequate instructions for each reader.

3. After Tien Pao responds to his mother's calls, continue the dialogue with the father's comments about a son who breaks a promise.

4. Tien Pao's lines about the money paid should follow the father's lecture. At that point more description should be skipped. Follow Tien Pao's explanation of the money he has earned with the mother's lines in which she communicates the worries she has had.

5. When the mother mentions the baby, write into the script the baby's name, Beauty of the Republic.

6. Omit the mother's references to the father's need to shop for food, but do include her asking Tien Pao to promise never to leave the riverbank again.

7. End the script as the mother says that all is well. Do not add her comment about the father's return.

NARRATOR'S CLOSING LINES:
However, Tien Pao does leave the riverbank again, but not because he wants to. The next day the sky is heavy with clouds, and great rains fall. So much rain falls that, when Tien Pao is napping, the sampan loosens from the mud bank and drifts down the river. Tien Pao awakens in the dark, and at first in his confusion and fear he shouts and calls. Realizing, however, that the Japanese and not his parents will hear him, he becomes quiet and begins to consider how he will survive alone in enemy territory and how he will find his parents.

MISSING

James Duffy

This script is from chapter 2, in which Sandy reports to the police that Kate is missing.

SUGGESTED STAGING:
The narrator stands at a lectern. Chief Torbert and Sandy sit in chairs.

	Chief Torbert	Sandy
	X	X
Narrator		
X		

NARRATOR'S OPENING LINES:

We are presenting a scene from *Missing* by James Duffy. The characters are Sandy, a worried twelve-year-old, read by _____, and a gruff policeman, Chief Torbert, read by _____. I, _____, am the narrator.

For the third time in two years Sandy has gone to Chief Torbert to report that her ten-year-old sister, Kate, is missing. The other times she was terrified with worry for her sister, but today she is only embarrassed. Wondering *why* Kate puts her through these ordeals, Sandy knocks at Chief Torbert's door, and a gruff voice orders her in.

SCRIPTING SUGGESTIONS:

1. Begin with the chief's first words. Instruct the chief's reader to use a gruff voice.

2. Omit movement and description.

3. At various points Sandy feels weak, dejected, and helpless. Instruct her reader to interpret those emotions.

4. After the chief tells Sandy that he has the description, insert the following lines for the narrator: His question is interrupted by the police radio. He turns up the radio and listens.

5. Follow the narrator's explanation with Chief Torbert's last words, and then end the script with the narrator's closing lines.

NARRATOR'S CLOSING LINES:

But Kate cannot find herself. Thrown into the back of a stranger's car, Kate has been kidnapped. The only hope for discovering the seriousness of Kate's predicament and for securing her safe release lies in Chief Torbert's recommendation that Sandy should check with Agatha Bates, a retired policewoman.

THE WHIPPING BOY

Sid Fleischman

This suggested script is taken from chapter 7 where the outlaws order the prince to write a ransom note.

SUGGESTED STAGING:

The narrator stands at a lectern. Prince Brat and Jemmy sit on the floor. Cutwater and Billy sit on stools.

Prince Brat   Jemmy

Billy   X   X   Cutwater

X   X

Narrator

X

NARRATOR'S OPENING LINES:

The scene we shall read is from *The Whipping Boy* by Sid Fleischman. The characters are spoiled Prince Brat, read by _____; Jemmy, the orphaned whipping boy, read by _____; and Hold-Your-Nose Billy and Cutwater, two outlaws, read by _____ and _____. I, _____, am the narrator.

Prince Brat is so spoiled that he refuses to learn to read or write. Whenever the Prince needs punishing, Jemmy, the orphaned whipping boy, receives it instead. One night Prince Brat orders Jemmy to run away with him. Jemmy is afraid because he knows that the king will hunt them down and *he,* not the prince, will be beaten. By dawn, they are lost in a fog and are captured in a forest by two outlaws. The stupid prince tells the outlaws that he is a prince, so they are taken to an old hut and ordered to write a ransom note.

SCRIPTING SUGGESTIONS:

1. Begin at the point where Cutwater finds a scrap of paper to give to Billy.

2. After Prince Brat confesses he cannot even scratch his name, let the narrator say: Jemmy gets an idea. He will pretend to be the prince and say Prince Brat is the whipping boy. If he can trick the outlaws, perhaps they will let the prince go and hold him instead.

3. Continue with Jemmy's speech in which he orders the outlaws to give him the quill.

4. Be sure to give Jemmy's reader the directions needed so he can act like the arrogant prince.

5. End the scene with Hold-Your-Nose Billy's lines in which he says to tell the king they are shameful men.

NARRATOR'S CLOSING LINES:

The outlaws are fooled, but Jemmy's plan backfires. Surprisingly, with the help of a hot-potato man, a girl named Betsy, and a dancing bear, the two boys reach safety. Even more surprising is the changed attitude of Prince Brat.

STONE FOX

John Reynolds Gardiner

This readers theatre presentation is taken from chapter 4, "The Reason," which is the chapter that explains what has made Grandfather sick.

SUGGESTED STAGING:

The narrator stands at a lectern. Little Willy and Clifford Snyder sit on stools.

Little Willy	Clifford Snyder
X	X

Narrator
X

NARRATOR'S OPENING LINES:

The scene that we are sharing is from *Stone Fox* by John Reynolds Gardiner. The characters are ten-year-old Little Willy, read by _____, and Clifford Snyder, a gruff stranger, read by _____. I, _____, am the narrator.

Little Willy is certain that some problem is making his grandfather ill. At first, Little Willy thinks that Grandfather is worried about harvesting the potatoes; but even after the potatoes are harvested and Grandfather has the money, he does not improve. Therefore, Little Willy knows that something else is bothering Grandfather. One night in early winter after Clifford Snyder has appeared on Grandfather's front porch, Little Willy finally understands what has been making Grandfather ill. As the scene opens, Little Willy's dog barks furiously at Clifford Snyder who is pointing a gun straight at the dog.

SCRIPTING SUGGESTIONS:

1. Although Grandfather is a silent participant in the chapter, leave him out of the script.

2. Begin the scene as Clifford Snyder orders Little Willy to move. Instruct the reader to deliver the line loudly and unkindly.

3. Omit movement and description.

4. When Clifford Snyder orders Little Willy to leave the dog outside, change "that *thing*" to "that *dog*."

5. After Clifford Snyder orders Little Willy into the house, insert the following lines for the narrator: Little Willy goes into the house without the dog, but Clifford Snyder does not put the gun away until they are in Grandfather's room, where he begins shouting at Grandfather.

6. Add "Old man'" to the beginning of Clifford Snyder's next lines so that the audience will understand that the grandfather is being addressed.

7. Skip the paragraph about Little Willy's combing Grandfather's hair, and add the next lines to Clifford Snyder's last speech.

8. Although the author explains Little Willy's confused thoughts about taxes and paying bills, write that paragraph as dialogue that Little Willy addresses to Clifford Snyder. Use "I" in place of "Little Willy," and change the verb forms to present tense.

9. Skip the part where Little Willy asks Grandfather if the tax problem is true.

10. After Little Willy asks Clifford Snyder whether he is sure, insert the following lines for the narrator: Little Willy stops speaking because he remembers the strongbox under the floorboards. He uncovers the box and takes the letters out.

11. Continue the scene until the end of the chapter.

NARRATOR'S CLOSING LINES:

Little Willy will find a way to pay the five hundred dollars because his grandfather has taught him that where there is a will, there is a way; and Little Willy has a will.

A MORGAN FOR MELINDA

Doris Gates

This suggested script is taken from chapter 2 where Dad, Mom, and Melinda talk to Mrs. Towers about a horse for Melinda.

SUGGESTED STAGING:

The narrator stands at a lectern. Mom, Dad, Melinda, and Mrs. Towers are sitting on stools.

```
                          Dad      Melinda
              Mom          X          X      Mrs. Towers
   Narrator    X                                   X
      X
```

NARRATOR'S OPENING LINES:

The scene that we have chosen is from *A Morgan for Melinda* by Doris Gates. The characters are Dad, a rural mail carrier, read by _____; ten-year-old Melinda, read by _____; her understanding Mom, read by _____; and the owner of Morgan Manor, Mrs. Towers, read by _____. I, _____, am the narrator.

Dad wants to buy a horse for his daughter, but Melinda really does not want a horse. However, after she sees the film *Justin Morgan Had a Horse,* she decides she will not mind having a horse if it is a Morgan. Although Dad assures Melinda that night that they cannot afford a Morgan, they decide to go to Morgan Manor on Sunday "just to look." Mrs. Tower, the owner, shows them around.

SCRIPTING SUGGESTIONS:

1. Begin at the point when Mrs. Towers smiles at Melinda and asks her if she wants a Morgan.

2. After Mrs. Towers says she definitely has a Morgan at that price, let her continue her speech about showing them Mantic Peter Frost. Leave out the speech about the barn.

3. After Mrs. Towers's speech let the narrator say: Melinda is excited about the little foal. He has big brown eyes and looks as friendly as a kitten.

4. Continue as Melinda asks her father to buy him.

5. Combine Dad's speech that the Morgan is cute with the one telling her she cannot ride him for two years.

6. End the scene with Dad's assurance to Mom that by the time Melinda would ride the registered Morgan, it would be broken and gentle.

NARRATOR'S CLOSING LINES:

Melinda's life changes when she gets the horse, and with the help of an elderly writer, Melinda begins to feel very special.

TO CATCH A CROOK

Dorothy Haas

This scene is taken from chapter 1 where the students discuss their school assignment.

SUGGESTED STAGING:
The narrator stands at a lectern. The four children sit on stools.

		Bucky		Justin	
	Gabby	X		X	Amy
Narrator	X				X
X					

NARRATOR'S OPENING LINES:

The scene we have chosen to read is taken from *To Catch a Crook* by Dorothy Haas. The characters are Gabby, who wants to be a private eye, read by _____; her friend Amy, who wants to be a veterinarian, read by _____; mischievous Justin, read by _____; and Justin's friend Bucky, read by _____. I, _____, am the narrator.

The teacher assigns career day reports from students on any profession they wish to choose. Gabby wants to be a private eye and Amy wants to be a veterinarian. The teacher suggests they use the Learning Media Center and also bring samples for their oral report. Gabby and Amy are discussing the assignment as they walk home from school. Bucky and Justin, who enjoy teasing the girls, are walking right behind them. Justin constantly irritates Gabby by saying, "Gotcha."

SCRIPTING SUGGESTIONS:

1. Begin with Gabby's speech that she does not need to go to the Learning Media Center. For audience understanding, use the complete words rather than LMC.

2. Be sure to give readers clues such as angrily, snickering, firmly, disgusted, etc.

3. After Justin says, "Gotcha," let Gabby say aloud to Amy that Justin is a pain.

4. Follow Gabby's speech with the following lines by the narrator: Bucky puts a felt-tip pen in front of Gabby as if it is a microphone and he is a news reporter.

5. Be sure to instruct Bucky to use a deep voice as he announces that he is Thomas Bucks.

6. Instead of having Porter pass by on his skateboard, let Justin say: "Did you hear what Porter is going to be? He wants to be an inventor. No wonder! He's a genius. Did you know he even put a motor on his skateboard."

7. Continue with Gabby's explanation that Porter took his dad's tape recorder apart.

8. End the scene as Gabby tells Justin that he can play the part of the dead body.

NARRATOR'S CLOSING LINES:

Much to Gabby's surprise her advertisement indicating that she solves mysteries nets her several customers. There seems to be a rash of puzzling disappearances. Surprisingly enough, all except one are solved by career day.

IN TROUBLE AGAIN, ZELDA HAMMERSMITH?

Lynn Hall

This suggested scene is taken from chapter 1 where Zelda causes Nathaniel to run his bike into a trash can.

SUGGESTED STAGING:

The narrator stands at a lectern. Zelda and Nathaniel sit on stools.

Zelda   Nathaniel

X   X

Narrator

X

NARRATOR'S OPENING LINES:

The scene we have chosen to read is from *In Trouble Again, Zelda Hammersmith?* by Lynn Hall. The characters are Zelda, a persistent fourth-grader, read by _____, and Nathaniel, a boy Zelda does not know but wants for a friend, read by _____. I, _____, am the narrator.

Zelda wants to become friends with a boy she has seen, so she spends the whole afternoon walking up and down the street. Finally, he comes out of his house, gets on his bike, and rides in her direction. She leaps in front of him, causing him to run into a trash can and fall off his bike.

SCRIPTING SUGGESTIONS:

1. Begin at the place where Zelda tells the boy her name and says she is his new girlfriend.

2. After the boy tells her to "bug off," let the narrator say: The boy gets back on his bike and starts away. Zelda runs along beside his bike, but it is hard to keep up a conversation when she is puffing for breath.

3. Continue by having Zelda ask the boy whether he already has a girlfriend.

4. After Zelda says she likes his dog, let the narrator say: The mention of his dog makes the boy stop pedaling.

5. Continue with the boy's answer that the dog is a purebred otter hound.

6. After Zelda says she has to know his whole name in order to send him valentines, direct Nathaniel to groan loudly in response.

7. Let the characters continue talking rather than having Nathaniel ride away.

8. End the scene with Nathaniel's speech telling Zelda to "bug off."

NARRATOR'S CLOSING LINES:

However, Zelda is determined to "bug on," but even the kidnapping she attempts does not work out as planned.

BRIGHTY OF THE GRAND CANYON

Marguerite Henry

This suggested script is the scene in which Jake Irons wanders into the old prospector's camp.

SUGGESTED STAGING:

The narrator stands at a lectern. Jake Irons and Old Timer sit on the floor.

Jake Irons   Old Timer

X   X

Narrator

X

NARRATOR'S OPENING LINES:

We shall read a scene from *Brighty of the Grand Canyon* by Marguerite Henry. The characters are Jake Irons, a treacherous beaver trapper, read by _____, and Old Timer, a generous, trusting old prospector, read by _____. I, _____, am the narrator.

Old Timer and his burro Brighty have returned to camp to celebrate their striking it rich by finding enough copper ore to last till kingdom come. As Old Timer is cooking flapjacks, a stranger named Jake Irons walks into camp carrying a beaver. Old Timer invites him to share the flapjacks so, after skinning the beaver, they start to eat. The trapper watches as Brighty takes a rolled pancake from Old Timer's hand and begins chewing it thoughtfully.

SCRIPTING SUGGESTIONS:

1. Begin as Jake Irons asks Old Timer in a scornful voice if the two of them always eat cakes and honey.

2. After Jake Irons says he likes his coffee that black, Old Timer can pretend to take a gold watch from his pocket. Begin his speech with "Guess I better wind my watch." Then continue with his saying, "It's only seven o'clock."

3. When Jake asks what they are celebrating, let Old Timer pause briefly, as if thinking. Then Jake can continue.

4. Be sure to give the readers clues in parentheses to the excited voice of Old Timer and the sarcastic one of Jake Irons.

5. After Old Timer comments on how rich the stuff is, let the narrator say: Old Timer gets up and spills the blue-flecked rocks into the greedy, outstretched hands of Jake Irons.

6. Continue as Jake asks where he found them.

7. Just let Jake hand back the nuggets to Old Timer rather than get up.

8. End the scene as Old Timer says that Brighty is a free spirit.

NARRATOR'S CLOSING LINES:

Old Timer does not get to reap the benefits from the strike. However, Brighty and Uncle Jim get to even the score—and some Grand Canyon guides say that on moonlight nights one can see the trail dust kicked up by a shaggy little beast—"Brighty himself, the roving spirit of the Grand Canyon—forever wild, forever free."

THE KELPIE'S PEARLS

Mollie Hunter

This script is from two scenes in chapter 1, "The Kelpie," in which Morag discovers a magical creature near her pond.

SUGGESTED STAGING:

The narrator stands at a lectern. The kelpie and Morag sit on stools.

Morag   Kelpie

X   X

Narrator

X

NARRATOR'S OPENING LINES:

Our readers theatre presentation is from *The Kelpie's Pearls* by Mollie Hunter. The characters are seventy-two-year-old Morag MacLeod, read by _____, and a magical creature known as a kelpie, read by _____. I, _____, am the narrator.

Morag lives alone on a small farm near Loch Ness in Scotland. One evening as she goes to her pond to get water, she hears a strange voice.

SCRIPTING SUGGESTIONS:

1. Begin the scene as the kelpie calls out to Morag.
2. Omit movement and description.
3. Before Morag asks who the kelpie is, have her say, "Well, there you are!"
4. As the two first meet, they snap at each other. Later they become more polite. Provide instructions so that the readers can communicate the emotions of the lines.
5. After the kelpie explains that he is caught between two stones, insert the following lines to be read by the narrator: Morag lifts the stone from the kelpie's foot, and he sits down, rubbing the pain away.
6. After Morag says that now she has seen a kelpie, insert the following lines for the narrator to read: Morag tells the kelpie good-night, and with her pail full of water she goes home. The following evening, as she returns for more water, she finds the kelpie sitting by the edge of the pond. He is skipping stones across the water.
7. Continue as Morag says that she has played the same game at the pool.
8. Change the kelpie's next lines to read: "Here, take this, and see whether you can skip a stone."
9. After the kelpie says, "Done!" insert the following lines for the narrator: And so Morag joins the kelpie in skipping stones. She enjoys playing with the kelpie; and when they finish, she again talks about her farm.
10. Continue with her description of her house.
11. End the scene as the kelpie says that he does not like being in Morag's debt.

NARRATOR'S CLOSING LINES:

Night after night Morag and the kelpie play skiffers; and therefore, night after night pearls are thrown into Morag's pond. Although she does not want them, Morag eventually owns a treasure of pearls which she never collects. However, the pearls cause Morag such a problem that in the end she depends on the kelpie to repay his debt in a splendid and magical way.

BLACKBERRIES IN THE DARK

Mavis Jukes

This suggested script is the scene in which Grandmother and Austin talk out in the barn near Grandfather's tractor.

SUGGESTED STAGING:

The narrator stands at a lectern. Grandmother and Austin sit on stools.

	Grandmother	Austin
	X	X
Narrator		
X		

NARRATOR'S OPENING LINES:

The scene that we shall read is from *Blackberries in the Dark* by Mavis Jukes. The characters are nine-year-old Austin, read by _____, and his grandmother, read by _____. I, _____, am the narrator.

Austin comes to visit his grandmother the year after his grandfather's death. Austin and his grandfather were such close friends and fishing buddies that Grandmother's heart aches for her sad grandson.

Austin has been invited by Wayne McCabe, a neighbor, to go fly-fishing but Austin refuses. Austin has never been fishing with anyone but his grandfather. Later, Austin's grandmother talks with him near Grandfather's workbench in the barn, with the fishing gear hanging nearby.

SCRIPTING SUGGESTIONS:

1. Begin with Grandmother's question about what Austin is thinking.

2. Combine Austin's speeches about blackberries, fly-fishing and the baseball cap.

3. Combine Grandmother's two speeches about nobody knowing it would be Grandfather's last summer and the one about the Yankees cap.

4. Do not have the character walk out as Austin asks his grandmother whether she is coming.

5. End the scene as Grandmother tells Austin not to cross any fences.

NARRATOR'S CLOSING LINES:

Grandmother and Austin combine blackberries and fly-fishing in a way that brings them closer and eases their sadness.

FROM THE MIXED-UP FILES OF MRS. BASIL E. FRANKWEILER

E. L. Konigsburg

This suggested script is taken from chapter 1 as Claudia talks to Jamie about running away.

SUGGESTED STAGING:

The narrator stands at a lectern. Claudia and Jamie are seated on chairs.

Claudia   Jamie

X   X

Narrator

X

NARRATOR'S OPENING LINES:

The characters for this scene from E. L. Konigsburg's *From the Mixed-Up Files of Mrs. Basil E. Frankweiler* are bored, "Straight A's" Claudia, read by _____, and her younger brother Jamie, read by _____. I, _____, am the narrator.

Claudia is dissatisfied with her life and plans to run away from monotony and injustice. As the scene opens, Jamie is angry at Claudia because she insists that he sit with her on the school bus. Jamie prefers to sit with his buddy Bruce and play cards.

SCRIPTING SUGGESTIONS:

1. Begin with Jamie's question as to why Claudia does not pick on Steve.

2. Give the reader clues about how Claudia is to speak, e.g., patiently, emphatically, etc.

3. Use the author's clues for how Jamie is to speak: pleading, muttering, impatiently, demanding, etc.

4. Omit the first mention of Claudia as she silently looks out the window, and combine Jamie's two speeches about picking on someone else and urging her to tell him as long as he is there.

5. Then give Claudia directions to quietly look away from Jamie as he angrily delivers his next two speeches.

6. Omit Jamie's thoughts as he feels flattered. Let him put his hand on his knee and pretend to be tough as he gives his O.K.

7. Avoid the description of Claudia's thoughts when Jamie whispers in a stage whisper that he has quite a bit of money. Let Jamie continue to his next speech without pausing.

8. After Jamie says he will never tell how he knows he will win, let Claudia put her thoughts into the following words: "I feel more certain than ever that I have chosen the right brother to escape with me. We complement each other perfectly. I am cautious and poor while you, Jamie, are adventurous and rich."

9. End the scene with Jamie's speech telling Claudia he knows what paper is made of.

NARRATOR'S CLOSING LINES:

Claudia and Jamie run away to a rather surprising place where they live in relative comfort and become involved in a very strange mystery.

RABBIT HILL

Robert Lawson

This suggested script is taken from chapter 1, "New Folks Coming."

SUGGESTED STAGING:

The narrator stands at a lectern. The character readers sit on stools.

		Mother	Father	
	Little Georgie	X	X	Porkey the Woodchuck
Narrator	X			X
X				

NARRATOR'S OPENING LINES:

Our readers theatre presentation is from *Rabbit Hill* by Robert Lawson. The characters are Little Georgie, a young rabbit, read by _____; his worried mother, read by _____; his father, a southern gentleman rabbit, read by _____; and a neighbor, Porkey the Woodchuck, read by _____. I, _____, am the narrator.

Little Georgie has heard the exciting news that is echoing all over Rabbit Hill, "New folks coming." He races home and tumbles down the burrow to tell his mother and father.

SCRIPTING SUGGESTIONS:

1. Begin as Little Georgie shouts the news to his mother and father. Be sure to instruct the reader to communicate Georgie's excitement.

2. Omit movement and description.

3. Provide instructions to remind the reader that Mother is a worrier.

4. After Father says that he is going for a walk to check on the rumor, insert the following lines for the narrator: As Father strolls over Rabbit Hill, he remembers the animals and the bountiful food that were once there. When he reaches the side lawn, he finds Porkey the Woodchuck. Porkey, thin and bedraggled, is fussing and grabbing mouthfuls of grass.

5. Follow those lines by the narrator with Porkey's complaint about the condition of the lawn.

6. Instruct the readers to communicate the doubt, the grumbling, and the hope that are found in the conversation between Father and Porkey the Woodchuck.

7. End the scene just before Father mentions bluegrass.

NARRATOR'S CLOSING LINES:

Father continues his stroll. He talks to the Fox, the Gray Squirrel, Willie the Fieldmouse, Phewie the Skunk, and the Deer. All of Rabbit Hill is buzzing with gossip and echoing the words, "New folks coming!"

A WRINKLE IN TIME

Madeleine L'Engle

This suggested script is from chapter 1. It is the scene in the kitchen of the Murry home just after the arrival of Mrs. Whatsit.

SUGGESTED STAGING:

The narrator stands at a lectern. Mrs. Whatsit, Mrs. Murry, Meg, and Charles Wallace are seated in chairs.

Mrs. Murry
Mrs. Whatsit   X
Narrator   X   Meg
X   X   Charles Wallace
                                     X

NARRATOR'S OPENING LINES:

We shall read a scene from *A Wrinkle in Time* by Madeleine L'Engle. The characters are Meg Murry, worried that she is unattractive and a poor student, read by _____; Charles Wallace, her quiet younger brother, read by _____; Mrs. Murry, their scientist mother, read by _____; and Mrs. Whatsit, a strange, agile old woman with extraordinary powers, read by _____. I, _____, am the narrator.

Charles Wallace is able to sense what Meg is thinking and to know when she is troubled. The absence of their father is unexplained, and their mother is trying to keep the family happy. As the scene opens, it is a wild, stormy night. Meg, hearing their dog barking above the howling wind, leaves her attic bedroom and goes to the kitchen where Charles Wallace is waiting for her. Mrs. Murry soon enters, and as they are eating, Charles Wallace tells them about Mrs. Whatsit and her two friends who live in an old, supposedly haunted house back in the woods. Just then, Fortinbras, the dog, growls at the outside laboratory door, and Mrs. Murry ushers in a bundled-up person wearing several scarves, a rough overcoat, and black rubber boots.

SCRIPTING SUGGESTIONS:

1. Begin with Charles Wallace's speech in which he suspiciously asks Mrs. Whatsit what she is doing there.

2. Omit the lines when Mrs. Murry asks Mrs. Whatsit to sit down. Let the audience assume she is already seated. Just let Mrs. Murry offer her a sandwich.

3. Omit Meg's speech offering to fix the tuna salad and going to the pantry. After Mrs. Whatsit meekly says, "All right," let her continue with her next speech about being in the neighborhood only a short time.

4. Avoid Meg's action at the refrigerator. Just let Mrs. Whatsit continue her speech about Mrs. Buncombe being able to spare sheets with the one asking Charles Wallace to tell Meg she's all right.

5. Also, leave out Meg's speech in which she offers Mrs. Whatsit the sandwich. Just combine Mrs. Whatsit's preceding speech with her asking to take off her boots.

6. After Mrs. Murry says she will help, let the narrator summarize the action by saying: As Mrs. Murry yanks on one slick boot it comes off suddenly and Mrs. Whatsit tumbles backward on the floor—chair and all. Water pours out of her boot and runs on the big braided rug.

7. After Mrs. Whatsit's speech about sprained dignity, let the narrator summarize again: Mrs. Whatsit scrambles up, rights her chair, and orders Mrs. Murry to remove the second boot. Then she contentedly finishes her sandwich, gets to her feet, and shakes her boots out over the sink.

8. Continue as Mrs. Whatsit says her stomach is full and it is time for her to go.

9. After Mrs. Whatsit repeats a second time that there *is* such a thing as a tesseract, let the narrator say: After putting on her boots and grabbing her shawls, Mrs. Whatsit hustles out the door.

10. Continue with Meg's worried speech to her mother.

11. End the scene with Mrs. Murry's loud stage whisper asking how Mrs. Whatsit could have known.

NARRATOR'S CLOSING LINES:

Meg discovers what tesseract means through a frightening experience in which love conquers. Meg becomes a new person who causes the family to be justly proud.

THE LION, THE WITCH AND THE WARDROBE

C. S. Lewis

This scene is from chapter 5, "Back on This Side of the Door," beginning with Peter and Susan's visit to the Professor's study

SUGGESTED STAGING:

The narrator stands at a lectern. The other readers sit on stools.

Susan
X

Peter   The Professor
X   X

Narrator
X

NARRATOR'S OPENING LINES:

We are sharing a scene from *The Lion, the Witch and the Wardrobe* by C.S. Lewis. The characters in this scene are an elder brother, Peter, read by _____; an elder sister, Susan, read by _____, and an old gentleman, known as the Professor, read by _____. I, _____, am the narrator.

Peter, Susan, and their younger brother and sister, whose names are Edmund and Lucy, have been sent from the London air raids of World War II to live in the country with the Professor. Almost immediately upon their arrival at the Professor's country home, Lucy, the youngest of the four, tells her brothers and sister about incredible adventures she is having in an old wardrobe, which she claims is the land of Narnia. Peter and Susan are concerned because Lucy appears to be out of her mind, and so they decide to tell the Professor. When they knock at the Professor's study door, he invites them in and finds chairs for them.

SCRIPTING SUGGESTIONS:

1. It will be necessary to write the first lines for the Professor, Peter, and Susan. Therefore, after the narrator's opening lines, include the following dialogue:

   THE PROFESSOR: Peter, Susan, you look worried. Is something troubling you?

   PETER: Yes, as a matter of fact, something strange and peculiar is going on. Lucy has told us about passing through an old wardrobe into a mysterious land called Narnia, which contains witches and other magical creatures.

   SUSAN: We know that it is all nonsense.

   PETER: Yes, of course, but Lucy's state of mind has not been helped by the fact that Edmund sometimes plays out the fantasy with her, but with us he denies that it is real.

   SUSAN: When Edmund says that Narnia is a pretend world, Lucy becomes very upset and angry.

   PETER: And that makes us think that there is really something wrong with Lucy. What do you think, Professor?

2. Continue the script with dialogue from the book. The next line should be that of the Professor as he asks Peter and Susan how they know the story is not true. Include instructions for the reader to portray the Professor as a serious man.

3. Provide instructions for Susan's and Peter's readers so that they can communicate the amazement and bewilderment those two experience after the Professor's logic suggests that there is a Narnia.

4. End the scene with the Professor's suggestion that they all mind their own business.

NARRATOR'S CLOSING LINES:

For several days nobody talks about the wardrobe, and Peter and Susan decide that things are better for Lucy. However, one day a large group of visitors comes to the Professor's home, and Peter, Susan, Edmund, and Lucy hide in the wardrobe. Almost immediately they discover that they are in the middle of a snow-covered forest, and Peter must apologize for not having believed Lucy. The adventures that follow are more wonderful and frightening than Peter and Susan could have imagined, and the Professor is left wondering, "What *do* they teach in schools today?"

MAIL-ORDER KID

Joyce McDonald

This suggested script from chapter 1 is the scene where Philip's mother and the fox are waiting for him when he arrives home from school.

SUGGESTED STAGING:

The narrator stands at a lectern. Mrs. Doty and Philip are sitting on chairs.

	Mrs. Doty	Philip
Narrator	X	X
X		

NARRATOR'S OPENING LINES:

We have chosen to read a scene from *Mail-Order Kid* by Joyce McDonald. The characters are Philip Doty, a fifth-grader, read by _____, and Mrs. Doty, a realtor and Philip's mother, read by _____. Todd, mentioned in the scene but not on stage, is Philip's adopted brother from Korea whom Philip resents deeply. I, _____, am the narrator.

Philip has ordered a fox through the mail without asking his parents' permission. As he arrives home from school one evening, his angry mother and the caged little fox are waiting for him. Philip decides to plead ignorance.

SCRIPTING SUGGESTIONS:

1. Begin with Philip's speech in which he asks his mother who sent the fox to them.

2. Make a speech out of Philip's thinking that his mother is talking about her children in a crummy way.

3. End the scene with Mrs. Doty's telling Philip that this is one of the weirdest stunts he has pulled in a long time.

NARRATOR'S CLOSING LINES:

Keeping a fox is not easy, and as time passes, Philip learns to accept his adopted brother. He realizes it is not easy to adapt to a new home.

SARAH, PLAIN AND TALL

Patricia MacLachlan

This suggested script is taken from chapters 1 and 2 in which Papa tells the children about Sarah and they find out that she plans to come.

SUGGESTED STAGING:

The narrator stands at a lectern. Papa, Anna, and Caleb sit on chairs.

                              Papa
                  Anna   X   Caleb
    Narrator   X   X
       X

NARRATOR'S OPENING LINES:

The scene that we shall share is taken from *Sarah, Plain and Tall* by Patricia MacLachlan. The characters are Caleb, a little boy who wants to hear about the mother he never knew, read by _____; his big sister Anna, who must care for their prairie home, read by _____; and Papa, their hard-working father, read by _____. I, _____, am the narrator.

Mama died the day after Caleb was born, and Caleb longs for the songs the family used to sing. One evening after supper he questions his father.

SCRIPTING SUGGESTIONS:

1. Begin the scene when Caleb asks his father why he does not sing anymore.

2. Have Papa add a bit to the speech in which he answers she would be a wife like Maggie. Make that speech read: "It is like our neighbor Maggie. You know Matthew wrote to ask for a wife and mother for his children, and she came from Tennessee."

3. Continue by having Papa pull a letter from his pocket, tell them he has an answer, and read it to them.

4. After Caleb says to ask Sarah whether she sings, have the narrator say: Caleb and Anna also write letters to Sarah. One morning in very early spring, as they are cleaning in the barn, Papa leans on his pitchfork and talks to the children.

5. Pick up the scene near the end of chapter 2 with Papa's speech in which he tells the children that Sarah will come for a month.

6. After the children respond and all are smiling, have the narrator say: Papa mails a letter to Sarah and sometime later receives a response.

7. Begin as Papa reads Sarah's short letter, which states she will arrive by train.

8. After Caleb asks Papa what is written at the bottom of the letter, end the scene as Papa reads Sarah's note to tell the children that she sings.

NARRATOR'S CLOSING LINES:

Sarah comes in the spring. The children want her to stay but are worried that she might miss the sea too much and leave. The days they share show the importance of home and a happy family.

WINNIE-THE-POOH

A. A. Milne

This scene is from chapter 9, "Piglet Is Entirely Surrounded by Water."

SUGGESTED STAGING:

The narrator stands at a lectern. Christopher Robin, Owl, and Winnie-the-Pooh sit on stools.

Christopher Robin
X

Owl   Winnie-the-Pooh
X   X

Narrator
X

NARRATOR'S OPENING LINES:

Our scene is from *Winnie-the-Pooh* by A.A. Milne. The characters are Christopher Robin, an adventurous boy, read by _____; Owl, read by _____; and the best bear in the world, Winnie-the-Pooh, read by _____. I, _____, am the narrator.

It has been raining for five days. Piglet's house is flooded, and Winnie-the-Pooh is able to travel only by floating on a corked-up honey jar. Christopher Robin, with his umbrella in one hand and a stick in the other, has gone outside to look around. While he is testing the depth of the water with his stick, Owl flies over.

SCRIPTING SUGGESTIONS:

1. Begin as Owl asks Christopher Robin how he is doing.

2. After Owl says that he will check on Pooh, insert the following line for the narrator: Owl flies off, and he returns very shortly.

3. Continue as Owl reports that Pooh is not there.

4. Omit the part where Pooh and Christopher hug.

5. End the scene after Pooh points out his boat.

NARRATOR'S CLOSING LINES:

Pooh is pointing to the corked-up honey jar, and both Pooh and Christopher agree that it will be impossible to rescue Piglet with such a boat. However, Pooh has the thought that Christopher's umbrella, when turned upside down, will make a fine boat. They name the new boat *Brain of Pooh,* and in it they float off to rescue Piglet.

THE SECRET LANGUAGE

Ursula Nordstrom

This suggested script is taken from chapter 1 where Victoria eats her first meal at Wingate Hall.

SUGGESTED STAGING:

The narrator stands at a lectern. Miss Mossman and the girls sit in chairs.

```
                              Eleanor    Victoria
                 Martha         X           X        Sue
    Narrator       X                                  X
       X                                         Miss Mossman
                                                      X
```

NARRATOR'S OPENING LINES:

In the scene we are sharing from Ursula Nordstrom's *The Secret Language* the characters are: Victoria, Coburn Boarding School's new student, read by _____; mischievous Martha, read by _____; Miss Mossman, the strict, ugly housemother, read by _____; and Sue and Eleanor, two other boarding school students, read by _____ and _____. I, _____, am the narrator.

Victoria is already homesick when she comes to eat her first meal at Wingate Hall. She is assigned to eat at the table of the housemother, Miss Mossman. Miss Mossman introduces her to the other girls.

SCRIPTING SUGGESTIONS:

1. Begin as Sue requests Victoria to repeat her name.

2. Be sure to give the instructions for the way the lines are to be read (e.g., loudly, scowling, insisting, etc.).

3. When appropriate, repeat the names of the girls as each speaker answers questions, in order to help the audience identify each speaker.

4. Divide the secret words into syllables as the author does to aid the reader in pronouncing each one.

5. Let Martha push back her chair and leave when Miss Mossman orders her to go to her room.

6. End the scene with Miss Mossman's command that Victoria look at her.

7. As the scene closes, Victoria cries silently while Eleanor and Sue giggle.

NARRATOR'S CLOSING LINES:

Martha and Victoria become friends. Victoria learns the secret language and is involved in a number of pranks inspired by Martha. By the end of the year the new housemother tells both girls that she will miss them during the summer and compliments them on how much they have learned during the year.

THE BORROWERS

Mary Norton

This suggested script is taken from chapter 1 where Mrs. May begins to tell Kate about the Borrowers.

SUGGESTED STAGING:
The narrator stands at a lectern. Mrs. May is seated in a chair, and Kate is seated on a stool.

	Mrs. May	Kate
Narrator	X	X
X		

NARRATOR'S OPENING LINES:
In the scene we are sharing from *The Borrowers* by Mary Norton, Kate, a young British girl, is read by _____, and Mrs. May is read by _____. I, _____, am the narrator.

As the scene opens, Kate and Mrs. May are together in Mrs. May's room so that Mrs. May can teach Kate how to crochet. Mrs. May lives in two rooms of Kate's parents' house.

SCRIPTING SUGGESTIONS:
1. Begin the scene with Mrs. May's lines in which she asks Kate if she has lost her tongue.

2. Omit the action of Mrs. May's brushing ashes under the grate when she tells about her brother.

3. Be sure to give clues to Kate's reader so she will act increasingly interested and excited as Mrs. May tells about her brother and the Borrowers.

4. End the scene with Kate's speech in which she begs Mrs. May to try to remember from the very beginning.

NARRATOR'S CLOSING LINES:
Tiny Arrietty, Pod, and Homily, who lived below the kitchen floor, become more and more believable as Mrs. May recounts her story. Arrietty's book becomes the final proof until Mrs. May tells about the way her brother made his *e*'s. Did the Borrowers really exist?

MRS. FRISBY AND THE RATS OF NIMH

Robert C. O'Brien

This suggested script from the chapter "The Crow and the Cat" is the scene where Mrs. Frisby checks with Jeremy, the crow, to see what to do about sick Timothy on moving day.

SUGGESTED STAGING:

The narrator stands at a lectern. Jeremy and Mrs. Frisby sit on the floor.

	Jeremy	Mrs. Frisby
Narrator	X	X
X		

NARRATOR'S OPENING LINES:

We shall read a scene from Robert O'Brien's *Mrs. Frisby and the Rats of NIMH* in which widowed Mrs. Frisby, the efficient field mouse, read by _____, is discussing a family problem with Jeremy, a crow, read by _____. I, _____, am the narrator.

In this scene Mrs. Frisby is very worried. Her son Timothy is too ill to be moved; and the family must leave their home in Farmer Fitzgibbon's garden before his sharp-bladed plow destroys them. Distraught, she decides to seek advice from Jeremy Crow, for whom she has earlier done a favor. Jeremy has just spied a piece of shiny foil and is picking it up.

SCRIPTING SUGGESTIONS:

1. Begin the scene as Mrs. Frisby asks Jeremy to wait.

2. Create a speech of explanation for Mrs. Frisby when Jeremy asks her to tell him what kind of help she needs. After she explains that the family has enough to eat, continue by having her say: "As you know it is time for moving day or the tractor and plow will tear up our garden home and kill us. However, little Timothy is too ill to move, and I do not know what to do."

3. Instruct Jeremy to move his head to one side and make a soft, sympathetic clucking sound as she tells her story.

4. After Jeremy offers to fly Mrs. Frisby to the owl's home, let Mrs. Frisby begin her speech in which she thanks him by saying her thoughts aloud. Begin with, "I have no choice."

5. When Jeremy says that the owl is out flying at night, have Mrs. Frisby act very nervous.

6. Close the scene as Jeremy promises Mrs. Frisby to be at her house at five o'clock.

NARRATOR'S CLOSING LINES:

Mr. Owl advises Mrs. Frisby to go see the rats who were friends of her respected dead husband, Jonathan. The rats tell her an amazing story, which she later repeats to her children from the safe home the rats help her create. The rats are gone now to be self-sufficient pioneers, but Mrs. Frisby's son Martin determines that someday he shall go to Thorn Valley and see them.

JACOB TWO-TWO MEETS THE HOODED FANG

Mordecai Richler

This script is taken from chapter 3, in which Jacob Two-Two suddenly finds himself in a strange and different world.

SUGGESTED STAGING:
The narrator stands at a lectern. Jacob Two-Two and Louis Loser sit on stools.

Jacob Two-Two

Narrator   X   Louis Loser

X   X

NARRATOR'S OPENING LINES:
We are sharing a scene from *Jacob Two-Two Meets the Hooded Fang* by Mordecai Richler. The characters are six-year-old Jacob Two-Two, read by _____, and a scruffy, skinny, and untidy man, Louis Loser, read by _____. I, _____, am the narrator.

Jacob Two-Two, the youngest in his family, has the habit of saying everything two times because no one ever hears him the first time. One day, while on a trip to the grocery store, Jacob Two-Two slips into a strange world, and he discovers that he is locked in a cell beneath a courthouse. A policeman appears and announces that before Jacob Two-Two faces the judge he may have one hour with his barrister (or attorney). Immediately Louis Loser, with his hair tangled and his clothes dirty, tumbles in. As the policeman introduces Mr. Loser, Jacob Two-Two decides that he is the messiest man he has ever seen.

SCRIPTING SUGGESTIONS:
1. Begin as Jacob Two-Two greets Mr. Loser.

2. Write twice those lines which the author indicates that Jacob says twice.

3. Omit all movement, including that of the policeman as he bangs on the door.

4. Provide instructions so that the readers will communicate the emotions that are described in the book. At different times Mr. Loser is astonished, thoughtful, triumphant, hopeful, pleased, enthralled, and delighted.

5. End the scene as Mr. Loser explains why he will plead insanity.

NARRATOR'S CLOSING LINES:
Two minutes later Jacob appears before the judge who charges him with having insulted a big person. Louis Loser does lose, and the next day Jacob Two-Two's adventures become even more curious and strange as he is carried to the children's prison where the warden is the Hooded Fang.

HOW TO EAT FRIED WORMS

Thomas Rockwell

This scene is taken from chapter 1, "The Bet," where Billy bets Alan fifty dollars that he can eat fifteen worms.

SUGGESTED STAGING:

The narrator stands at a lectern. Alan and Tom sit in chairs, and Billy and Joe sit on the floor.

        Tom   Billy

Alan   X   X   Joe

X   X

Narrator

X

NARRATOR'S OPENING LINES:

We are sharing the opening scene from *How to Eat Fried Worms* by Thomas Rockwell. The characters in this scene are Tom, a lanky, serious boy, read by _____; nervous and argumentative Alan, read by _____; spunky and freckled-faced Billy, read by _____; and Joe, a small boy, read by _____. I, _____, am the narrator.

Alan and Billy are walking down the sidewalk, and they stop to talk with Tom who is sitting on his front porch. Joe joins them later.

SCRIPTING SUGGESTIONS:

1. Begin the presentation with the first line of the book. Assign the first line to Alan and the second one to Billy.

2. Assign the lines that tell about Old Man Tator to Alan and those that tell about Joe's mother to Billy.

3. Alan asks Tom where he was and continues with questions about his being kept in.

4. Omit description and references to movement.

5. During the scene several questions are directed to specific individuals; therefore it will be necessary to have the reader address the person to whom the lines are spoken. For example, have Alan say, "Billy, how about mud?" rather than "How about mud?"

6. After Tom says that he would not eat fifteen worms, have the narrator read the following line: Joe walks down the sidewalk and sits in the grass beside Billy.

7. End the scene at the end of the chapter.

NARRATOR'S CLOSING LINES:

Billy takes the bet because he will do almost anything for fifty dollars and because he eats almost anything—fried liver, pig's feet, mushrooms, tongue. His usual problem is finding enough to eat. However, it takes more than a good appetite and the hope of a new minibike to help him swallow the first bite of night crawler.

WORDS BY HEART

Ouida Sebestyen

This suggested scene is taken from the end of chapter 2, which contains the account of the Sills family who returns home to find that someone has been in their home.

SUGGESTED STAGING:

The narrator stands at a lectern. Lena, Ben, and Claudie sit on stools.

```
                              Lena
                   Ben         X              Claudie
     Narrator       X                            X
        X
```

NARRATOR'S OPENING LINES:

Our readers theatre presentation is from *Words by Heart* by Ouida Sebestyen. The characters are members of the Sills family, a black family living in rural America. The characters are Lena, a bright and sensitive daughter, read by _____; Ben, her wise father, read by _____; and Claudie, her stepmother, read by _____. I, _____, am the narrator.

On this summer night the Sills family has just returned home from church where Lena has won a contest for being able to quote the most scriptures from the Bible. It has been a difficult evening. Lena knew she had entered the contest without the support of others in the church, and the prize was a blue bow tie, which told her that nobody expected her to win. However, the worst part of the evening is waiting for the family when they return home. A butcher knife, having passed through a loaf of bread and the tablecloth, is stuck vertically into the table. Lena and Claudie see the knife first, and they call Ben. He comes running.

SCRIPTING SUGGESTIONS:

1. Begin with Ben's question of whether the butcher knife is all that is wrong. Instruct the reader to show that Ben is out of breath from running and that he is afraid.

2. At the point where Claudie leaves the room, insert the following lines for the narrator: Then Claudie turns and runs from the room. Pa works the knife free from the table and slowly puts it back in the drawer.

3. Continue as Lena asks whether she should have won.

4. Skip the part in which Lena sits on Ben's lap. This adaptation will necessitate combining Ben's lines that precede and follow that action.

5. Omit movement and description.

6. End the scene with Ben's statement that people should always strive to be better than themselves, not better than someone else.

NARRATOR'S CLOSING LINES:

The intruder is not to be forgotten. He becomes a tragic part of the Sills family, and the hardest thing that Lena will ever do is to follow Ben's example and return evil not with evil, but with good.

THE CRICKET IN TIMES SQUARE

George Selden

This suggested script is taken from chapter 3 in which Chester Cricket and Tucker Mouse become acquainted.

SUGGESTED STAGING:
The narrator stands at a lectern. Chester and Tucker sit on stools.

	Chester	Tucker
Narrator	X	X
X		

NARRATOR'S OPENING LINES:
We shall read a scene from George Selden's *The Cricket in Times Square.* Chester Cricket, frightened and hungry, is read by _____. Tucker Mouse, who saves everything, is read by _____. I, _____, am the narrator.

As the story begins, Mario Bellini, who is trying to sell papers in his father's newsstand at the Times Square subway station, hears a weak sound rising from a pile of waste paper and soot. He finds a little cricket, and after much persuasion his parents let him keep it in a matchbox on a shelf. That night Tucker Mouse, who lives in a drain pipe, climbs on a stool and calls to Chester.

SCRIPTING SUGGESTIONS:
1. Begin the scene with Tucker's loud whisper calling to see whether Chester is awake. When Chester does not answer, instruct Tucker to pause only briefly before trying again to attract his attention.

2. After Chester agrees to let Tucker come up, let the narrator say: Tucker jumps to the shelf and looks at Chester admiringly.

3. When Chester says it is a long story, let Tucker sigh happily as he asks Chester to tell him. Add to Tucker's speech the lines: "I love to hear stories. It is almost as much fun as eavesdropping if the story is true."

4. Tucker finds out that Chester likes liverwurst and tells him to wait. Then let the narrator describe the action as follows: Tucker leaps to the floor, dashes to the drain pipe, and after rummaging around, finds a big piece of liverwurst he had stored away earlier. He returns with it to Chester's shelf where Chester decides that Tucker is a very excitable but generous mouse.

5. Be sure to instruct Tucker's reader to moan with pleasure as Chester describes the picnic basket.

6. Give the readers clues in parentheses to the ways to share the lines, i.e., sympathetically, exclaiming, forlornly, etc.

7. End the scene as Chester says that he chirped because he needed to do something.

NARRATOR'S CLOSING LINES:
In the weeks that follow, Chester Cricket becomes famous, but he still longs for Connecticut. And as the story ends, Tucker Mouse and Harry Cat are planning a trip to the country.

STINKER FROM SPACE

Pamela Service

This suggested script is from chapters 2 and 3 in which Tsyng Yr meets Karen for the first time.

SUGGESTED STAGING:

The narrator stands at a lectern. Tsyng Yr and Karen are seated on the floor.

	Karen	Tsyng Yr
	X	X
Narrator		
X		

NARRATOR'S OPENING LINES:

We shall read a scene from *Stinker from Space* by Pamela Service. One of the characters is Tsyng Yr, read by _____. He is an agent of the Sylon Confederacy in Outer Space, who will speak the lines aloud that he communicates through his thoughts. The other character is Karen, a young girl, read by _____. She loves to imagine adventures in great interstellar dramas. I, _____, am the narrator.

Tsyng Yr's spaceship crashes in a hidden clearing and, in order not to die, he transfers his mind into the only animal in sight, a skunk. Hungry, and a bit bewildered, he comes upon Karen, seated under a maple tree playing with Dark Destroyer and other action characters in great interstellar dramas. Tsyng Yr discovers that his new body does not have speech ability so he communicates with a surprised Karen through his thoughts.

SCRIPTING SUGGESTIONS:

1. Begin the scene by having Tsyng Yr tell Karen his thoughts that he is dreadfully hungry.

2. Let Karen and Stinker speak aloud their thoughts to each other.

3. Let the narrator speak the following lines after Tsyng Yr lets Karen know he was the one asking for the sandwich: Karen is surprised, then alarmed, but she is afraid to make a sudden move that would startle the skunk into stinking on her.

4. Continue with Tsyng Yr's indignant remark that he would not stink on her.

5. Instead of having Karen say, "Here," as she throws a cookie to Tsyng Yr, have her say, "Here, eat this."

6. Omit the action of the skunk's waddling around.

7. After Tsyng Yr admits that his body seems to be constantly hungry, let the narrator fill in the action with the following lines: Karen stands and slowly walks across the clearing with the skunk following her eagerly. Suddenly she turns and looks at her strange companion.

8. End the scene by having Karen laughingly say that his name is perfect.

NARRATOR'S CLOSING LINES:

Tsyng Yr convinces Karen and her computer-buff friend Jonathan that he must return to his planet with valuable military information. How can they help him?

MOVING IN

Alfred Slote

The following script is from chapter 2.

SUGGESTED STAGING:

The narrator stands at a lectern. Dad, Robby, and Peggy sit on stools.

		Dad	
	Robby	X	Peggy
Narrator	X		X
X			

NARRATOR'S OPENING LINES:

This readers theatre presentation is from the second chapter of *Moving In* by Alfred Slote. The characters in this scene are eleven-year-old Robby, read by _____; his pushy thirteen-year-old sister, Peggy, read by _____; and his widowed father, Mr. Miller, read by _____. I, _____, am the narrator.

The Millers have moved three times that Robby can remember; and although he does not want to move again, he, his dad, and his sister are on their way from Boston to Arborville, Michigan, where his dad has accepted a new position. They have combined the move with a vacation by traveling the long way through Canada and by camping out in parks. In this scene the three are sitting around a campfire. Dad is drinking coffee, and Robby and Peggy are looking into the flames.

SCRIPTING SUGGESTIONS:

1. Begin at the point where Dad says that they will begin a new chapter tomorrow.

2. Include clues for the readers so that they understand that Dad patiently ignores his children's negative feelings, that Robby is angry over the move, and that Peggy is suspicious and prying.

3. Omit description and movement.

4. Rewrite the long paragraph that explains why Dad offered to buy Computel. Shorten it, and change the point of view so that the new lines may be read by Dad.

5. Substitute "our housekeeper" for "Mrs. O'Rourke" and "our friends" for "Monk Kelly."

6. End the scene with Dad's comment that he does not see why Computel cannot sponsor a baseball team.

NARRATOR'S CLOSING LINES:

The thought that Computel could sponsor a baseball team pleases Robby, and he begins to concentrate on the marshmallows. Peggy, however, takes the new information about Arborville and decides that the partner, Ruth Lowenfeld, has plans to marry Dad. By the time that Peggy and Robby arrive in Arborville, they are determined to thwart the romance. Although some of their plans produce ridiculous results, others are so dangerous that they threaten to destroy not only Computel but also the Miller family.

THE SIGN OF THE BEAVER

Elizabeth Speare

This suggested script is taken from chapter 3 where the heavyset, bearded stranger arrives at the cabin.

SUGGESTED STAGING:

The narrator stands at a lectern. Matt and the stranger sit on stools.

Matt   Stranger

X   X

Narrator

X

NARRATOR'S OPENING LINES:

We shall read a scene from *The Sign of the Beaver* by Elizabeth Speare. The characters are Matt, a thirteen-year-old boy, read by _____, and a heavyset, frightening, bearded stranger, read by _____. I, _____, am the narrator.

Matt has been left alone to guard his family's newly built cabin in Maine territory. A few days after his father has gone back to Massachusetts to get the rest of the family, Matt is sitting in front of the open cabin door when a suspicious stranger wearing a ragged blue army coat walks to the door. Matt feels uneasy as the stranger peers into the empty cabin.

SCRIPTING SUGGESTIONS:

1. Begin with the stranger's questioning whether Matt is alone.

2. Change the speech about the rifle slightly so the audience will know what the stranger is looking at. Instead of his saying, "Mighty fine piece," let him say, "That's a fine-looking rifle hanging over the door." Then add the line about beaver.

3. After Matt replies that his father will not sell the rifle, add the following narrator speech: Matt fixes corn cake and stew for supper, and before the stranger finishes eating, he has wolfed down every last bite.

4. Let the stranger continue by telling Matt that it was a tasty supper.

5. Combine the stranger's speech about keeping away till things quiet down with his next lines.

6. After the stranger says he can bed down anywhere, let the narrator speak by saying: As the stranger sprawls on the floor with his back against a wall, it looks as if he is planning to spend the night even though Matt has not invited him.

7. Continue by combining the stranger's speech about tobacco with the one about when he was a boy.

8. After Matt asks him if the Indians speak English, combine the stranger's next three speeches and end the scene.

NARRATOR'S CLOSING LINES:

The stranger falls asleep, and Matt is worried. Is the stranger a murderer? Matt determines to stay awake but cannot do so. In the morning when he awakens, the stranger is gone and so is his father's rifle. Matt now has no way to shoot game or to protect himself. In the weeks that follow, a proud Indian boy teaches Matt how to survive, and gives him a lasting respect for the Indian way of life.

A DOG ON BARKHAM STREET

Mary Stolz

This suggested script is taken from chapter 1 in which Edward talks to his mother about bullies.

SUGGESTED STAGING:
The narrator stands at a lectern. Edward and his mother, Mrs. Frost, sit in chairs.

	Edward	Mrs. Frost
	X	X
Narrator		
X		

NARRATOR'S OPENING LINES:

In the scene we are sharing from Mary Stolz's *A Dog On Barkham Street,* a very discouraged Edward Frost, read by _____, is talking with his sympathetic mother, read by _____. I, _____, am the narrator.

Edward Frost has two problems. He wants a dog desperately, but his parents refuse because Edward so rarely accepts family responsibility. His more immediate problem is his fear of Martin Hastings, the bully of Barkham Street who lives next door. Edward just cannot seem to avoid Martin.

SCRIPTING SUGGESTIONS:

1. Begin the scene at the point where Edward asks his mother why Dad does not get a job in Alaska.

2. Have Mrs. Frost answer Edward's question as follows: "You know your father teaches at the university. He couldn't very easily change his position just like that."

3. When Mrs. Frost questions Edward about what Martin did this time, let Edward's response be: "This time Martin chased me for blocks. When I was so tired I fell down, he sat on top of me, pulled my hair, and made me say 'uncle.' Now he says I have to say 'uncle' whenever he wiggles his finger at me."

4. Let Mrs. Frost reply, "I'm sorry, Edward."

5. Continue by having Edward say he is going to get a crew cut.

6. After Mrs. Frost asks Edward how he can stand up to someone twice his size, continue Edward's reply with: "The trouble is, if you are going to stand up to somebody, you have to remember to stand still. I always forget and run."

7. Let that speech close the scene.

NARRATOR'S CLOSING LINES:

Edward's problems continue, but he finally solves one with the assistance of an understanding hobo, Uncle Josh.

JOURNEY TO TOPAZ

Yoshiko Uchida

This suggested script is from chapter 1, "Strangers at the Door." The presentation combines two scenes: the one where Yuki's family is at the dinner table and the other where Yuki's father is taken away.

SUGGESTED STAGING:

The narrator stands at a lectern. Father, Mother, and Yuki sit in chairs. The FBI agent sits on a stool, and the radio newscaster sits on the floor.

```
                        Mother        Yuki
                          X            X
              Father                         FBI Agent
                X                               X
    Narrator                                        Radio Newscaster
       X                                                  X
```

NARRATOR'S OPENING LINES:

Our readers theatre presentation is from *Journey to Topaz* by Yoshiko Uchida. The characters are eleven-year-old Yuki, read by _____; her father, a quiet man, read by _____; her mother, a tense woman, read by _____; and an FBI agent, read by _____. Reading the radio news bulletin is _____. I, _____, am the narrator.

Journey to Topaz, the story of a Japanese-American family, is set during World War II in northern California. As this scene opens, Yuki and her mother and father are having dinner. They are puzzled by a radio announcement, and later they are startled as an FBI agent rings the doorbell.

SCRIPTING SUGGESTIONS:

1. Although three FBI agents and two policemen come to the house, for a simpler reading only one agent appears in the suggested staging.

2. Begin the scene with the reading of the radio news bulletin.

3. As the scene opens, provide instructions for Yuki calmly to look at her mother and father, for the father to appear in intense thought, and for the mother to frown with worry. The reading of the mother's lines will later need to communicate her increasing nervousness.

4. Omit all movement.

5. Skip the section about the telephone call.

6. Do not indicate that any time has passed from the conversation at the dinner table until the arrival of the FBI agent.

7. After Father offers the suggestion that perhaps the bulletin has been a drama, insert the following narrator's lines: At this point the doorbell rings. Father leaves and then returns with the FBI agent.

8. Follow those lines with father's explanation of the gentleman's identity. Adapt those lines so that Father explains the appearance of only one man. Instruct the reader to communicate Father's tenseness. (Several paragraphs will be skipped.)

9. Give all the lines spoken by the various law enforcement officers to the FBI agent.

10. End the scene as Father asks the family not to worry.

NARRATOR'S CLOSING LINES:

However, Yuki's family has every reason to worry. It will be many months before they are together again as a family. They will lose almost all of their possessions, and Ken, Mother, and Yuki will be imprisoned first in a horse barn at a race track and then later in barracks on the barren Topaz Desert in Utah. Theirs is a story of confusion and tragedy and courage, told honestly and vividly by an author who lived through the evacuation of Japanese-Americans.

A DOG CALLED KITTY

Bill Wallace

This scene is taken from chapter 3 where Ricky explains to Brad why he is afraid of dogs.

SUGGESTED STAGING:

The narrator stands at a lectern. Brad and Ricky sit on stools.

Brad   Ricky

X   X

Narrator

X

NARRATOR'S OPENING LINES:

The scene we have chosen to read is from Bill Wallace's *A Dog Called Kitty*. The characters are dog-fearing Ricky, read by _____, and Brad, his concerned best friend, read by _____. I, _____, am the narrator.

The boys have been playing football, without permission, at the high school football stadium. Ricky catches the ball in the end zone and makes a touchdown. Sammy, a bully, hits him late, and knocks the ball away. Everyone except Sammy agrees it is a touchdown. He pushes Ricky into the sprinklers and challenges him to a fight. Ricky has the fight won when Sammy's dog begins barking and Ricky runs. Somehow, Ricky gets on top of the fence behind the bleachers and that is where Brad finds him. The dog is still barking but runs away when it sees Brad act as if he is picking up a rock.

SCRIPTING SUGGESTIONS:

1. Begin with Brad's explanation that the dog is as big a coward as Sammy. Continue with Brad's next speech without a response from Ricky.

2. Let Ricky respond to Brad's question about why he ran with a tearful answer: "Just go away."

3. After Brad tells Ricky the dog is gone, have Ricky look all around fearfully without speaking. Then let Brad continue with his next lines.

4. After Ricky tells Brad that he will come down, let the narrator say: Brad helps Ricky off the fence, and after waiting for workmen to leave, they sit down on the top step of the bleachers.

5. Let Brad continue with his speech in which he asks Ricky to tell him what happened. Without a response from Ricky, follow with Brad's lines saying that perhaps he can help.

6. Let Ricky give his first speech about the dog biting him.

7. When Ricky closes his eyes and shudders, give Brad a speech saying sympathetically, "Go on."

8. Summarize the rest of Ricky's story, leaving out some of the description.

9. Follow with Ricky's sigh and his speech about how awful it was.

10. End the scene with Ricky's telling Brad just to forget it.

NARRATOR'S CLOSING LINES:

Ricky's problem is very real, and it takes a homeless pup to help him overcome it.

CHARLOTTE'S WEB
E. B. White

This suggested script is from chapter 7, "Bad News," in which Wilbur learns why he is being fattened up.

SUGGESTED STAGING:
The narrator stands at a lectern. Charlotte, Wilbur, Fern, and the old sheep sit on stools.

		Wilbur	Fern	
	Charlotte	X	X	The old sheep
Narrator	X			X
X				

NARRATOR'S OPENING LINES:
The scene we are sharing is from *Charlotte's Web* by E.B. White. The characters in this scene are Charlotte, a spider and Wilbur's loyal friend, read by _____; Wilbur, a young and immature pig, read by _____; Fern, a little girl who is Wilbur's caretaker, read by _____; and the old sheep, read by _____. I, _____, am the narrator.

Wilbur has grown larger and fatter since Fern sold him to Mr. Zuckerman. He enjoys spending long hours sleeping and dreaming in Zuckerman's barn. On this particular afternoon Fern, Charlotte, and the old sheep are visiting with him.

SUGGESTIONS FOR SCRIPTING:

1. Begin the scene with the old sheep's comment that Wilbur is putting on weight.

2. Although Fern does not have a speaking part, she should hold a script, and she should be given instructions to react to the bad news. For example, when Wilbur first screams, Fern sits rigidly on her stool.

3. Wilbur screams and cries with fear, and the reader should be given instructions to interpret his lines with great emotion.

4. Charlotte is brisk and confident, and her reader should be given clues for interpreting her lines.

5. The old sheep is gruff, and at the end of the scene she is snapping at Wilbur. Those clues for interpreting her personality should be given to her reader.

6. End the scene with Charlotte's comment that she cannot stand hysterics.

NARRATOR'S CLOSING LINES:
Wilbur likes Charlotte. He appreciates her sensible and useful campaign against flies. However, in the months to come Charlotte will grow into a warm and true friend even more resourceful than those in the barn can imagine.

LITTLE HOUSE ON THE PRAIRIE

Laura Ingalls Wilder

This recommended scene is from chapter 7, "The Wolf-pack," which recounts the time fifty wolves appeared on the Ingalls homestead.

SUGGESTED STAGING:

The narrator stands at a lectern. Pa, Ma, and Laura sit on stools.

```
                            Pa
                Ma          X        Laura
   Narrator      X                     X
      X
```

NARRATOR'S OPENING LINES:

This readers theatre presentation is taken from *Little House on the Prairie* by Laura Ingalls Wilder. The characters in this scene are Laura Ingalls, read by _____; her pa, Charles Ingalls, read by _____; and her ma, Caroline Ingalls, read by _____. I, _____, am the narrator.

In this book the Ingalls family moves from the Big Woods of Wisconsin and settles on a homestead near the Verdigris River in Indian Territory. One day Pa is late returning home. When Ma finally sees him riding across the prairie, Patti, the horse, is stretched out in a full gallop, and Pa is leaning forward nearly flat on the horse's back. Patti races past the stable, and Pa finally brings her to a halt. She is shaking, and both she and Pa are breathless.

SCRIPTING SUGGESTIONS:

1. Begin the scene as Ma asks Pa what is wrong.

2. Provide instructions so that Ma's reader will communicate the concern that Ma feels for Pa.

3. Before Ma repeats her question, provide instructions so that Pa's reader knows to breathe hard and to look back over his shoulder. Pa's reader will need clues to remain breathless for several lines.

4. Omit the description and dialogue that follow Pa's explanation that fifty wolves chased him over the prairie. Continue the script at the point several pages later when Pa begins to explain that it was the biggest wolf-pack he has ever seen.

5. End the scene with Ma's telling the girls that it is time for bed. Give instructions for that line to be read cheerfully.

NARRATOR'S CLOSING LINES:

However, that is not the end of the wolf-pack. That night the wolves surround the little cabin. While the howls of fifty wolves echo across the prairie, Patti squeals from the barn, and the bulldog growls and paces in front of the quilt that is the Ingalls's front door. Pa holds Laura up to the window so that she can see the circle of shaggy gray wolves with glimmering green eyes. Finally, with Pa and the bulldog to guard the cabin, Laura goes to sleep.

Appendixes

APPENDIX A

BIBLIOGRAPHY
OF COMPLETED SCRIPTS

Alcott, Louisa May. *Little Women; or, Meg, Jo, Beth and Amy.* Boston: Little, Brown, 1868.
   The lives of Meg, Jo, Beth, and Amy give a picture of early New England family life.

Baum, L. Frank. *The Wonderful Wizard of Oz.* Illus. by W.W. Denslow. Chicago: G.M. Hill, 1900.
   All wishes are finally granted after Dorothy and her strange companions make the trip to the Emerald City.

Burnett, Frances Hodgson. *The Secret Garden.* New York: Grosset & Dunlap, 1911.
   Mary Lennox, an orphan, is sent to live with her uncle at Misselthwaite, an old estate in Yorkshire, where she discovers a secret garden and an invalid cousin who, by joining her efforts to restore the garden to beauty, gains his health and his father's attention.

Carroll, Lewis. *Alice's Adventures in Wonderland.* Illus. by John Tenniel. New York: Macmillan, 1866.
   Alice has a series of fantastic experiences with surprising characters that she meets after she follows a rabbit down his hole.

Dickens, Charles. *A Christmas Carol.* Illus. by Frank Bindley. London: M. Ward, 189-.
   After dreaming of Christmases past, future, and present, Ebenezer Scrooge discovers the true meaning of Christmas.

Dodge, Mary Mapes. *Hans Brinker, or the Silver Skates, A Story of Life in Holland.* Illus. by F.O.C. Darley and Thomas Nast. New York: James O'Kane, 1866.
   A competition for silver skates and the help of a doctor in restoring their father's memory change the lives of Hans and Gretel.

Grimm, Jacob and Wilhelm. *Grimm's Household Tales,* 2 volumes. London: George Bell, 1884.
   The stories "The Water of Life" and "One-Eye, Two-Eyes, and Three-Eyes" are included in this collection.

Kipling, Rudyard. *Just So Stories for Little Children.* Illus. by author. New York: Doubleday, Page, 1902.
   This collection contains twelve humorous stories, including "How the Camel Got His Hump."

Spyri, Johanna. *Heidi.* Trans. by Helen B. Dole. Boston: Ginn & Co., 1899.
   Heidi, an orphan, finds happiness at her grandfather's alpine cottage where she lives, eats, and plays simply.

Stevenson, Robert Louis. *Treasure Island*. New York: Scribner, 1896.

    Jim Hawkins, after discovering a treasure map in an old pirate's chest, shares it with Dr. Livesey and Squire Trelawney who outfit a ship and sail for Treasure Island, only later to discover that Long John Silver and other pirates are members of the crew.

Wiggin, Kate Douglas Smith. *Rebecca of Sunnybrook Farm*. Boston: Houghton Mifflin, 1903.

    Happy, positive Rebecca touches the lives of the two maiden aunts with whom she comes to live.

APPENDIX B

BIBLIOGRAPHY
OF SUGGESTED SCRIPTS

Anderson, Margaret J. *The Journey of the Shadow Bairns.* Illus. by Patricia Lincoln. New York: Knopf, 1980.
   After her parents' sudden death, a brave thirteen-year-old Scottish girl takes her four-year-old brother on a one-way trip to Canada where her family had planned to relocate.

Arnosky, Jim. *Gray Boy.* New York: Lothrop, Lee & Shepard, 1988.
   Thirteen-year-old Ian raised Gray Boy from a puppy, but he must now face the threat that the dog is potentially dangerous.

Atwater, Richard and Florence. *Mr. Popper's Penguins.* Illus. by Robert Lawson. Boston: Little, Brown, 1938.
   A penguin sent to a painter who dreamed of polar expeditions changes the lives of the Popper family.

Babbitt, Natalie. *Tuck Everlasting.* New York: Farrar, Straus & Giroux, 1975.
   Winnie Foster finds the Tuck family's secret spring that gives those who drink from it immortality, and she must discover not only the meaning of "everlasting" but also how to protect the Tucks.

Brittain, Bill. *Who Knew There'd Be Ghosts?* Illus. by Michele Chessare. New York: Harper & Row, 1985.
   Through Tommy, Books, and Harry the Blimp's effort to save the old Parnell House, their favorite place to play, they discover unexpected allies—two ghosts who help them to unravel the mystery and to locate a valuable document.

_____. *The Wish Giver.* Illus. by Andrew Glass. New York: Harper & Row, 1983.
   Thaddeus Blinn grants each of four characters the fulfillment of a wish, three of which are interpreted in a surprisingly literal way.

Bulla, Clyde Robert. *Shoeshine Girl.* Illus. by Leigh Grant. New York: Crowell, 1975.
   Willful ten-year-old Sara Ida is sent to live with her aunt for a summer, and, deprived of an allowance, she defiantly takes a job as a shoeshine girl; in the process she learns to be less self-centered.

Burch, Robert. *Ida Early Comes Over the Mountain.* New York: Viking, 1980.
   Ida has a gentle, humorous approach to being the Sutton housekeeper and teaches the older children the meaning of true friendship.

Butterworth, Oliver. *The Enormous Egg*. Illus. by Louis Darling. Boston: Little, Brown, 1956.
Nate Twitchell's life is changed drastically when a dinosaur hatches out of a leathery-shelled egg.

Byars, Betsy. *After the Goat Man*. Illus. by Ronald Himler. New York: Viking, 1974.
As Harold helps Figgy and his grandfather, he begins to overcome his own problems.

———. *The Animal, the Vegetable, and John D. Jones*. Illus. by Ruth Sanderson. New York: Delacorte, 1982.
Denise and Clara expect a miserable summer vacation when their father includes Delores Jones and her son John; however, a near tragedy causes them to alter their values and attitudes.

———. *The Blossoms Meet the Vulture Lady*. Illus. by Jacqueline Rogers. New York: Delacorte, 1986.
Junior, accidentally caught in his own coyote trap, is rescued by Mad Mary; and, although his family is frantic, he has a great adventure as Mary's prisoner.

———. *The Burning Questions of Bingo Brown*. New York: Viking, 1988.
Having more questions than answers, Bingo decides to keep a journal not of observations but of questions, which include topics that focus on the stability of a disturbed teacher, the techniques of mixed-sex phone conversations, the motives of the class bully, and other problems, both wacky and serious.

———. *Cracker Jackson*. New York: Viking, 1985.
Cracker Jackson attempts to save his ex-baby sitter Alma from her husband who is abusing her.

———. *The Cybil War*. Illus. by Gail Owens. New York: Viking, 1981.
Simon and Tony are both in love with Cybil, a fourth-grade classmate; and because Tony uses lies to strengthen his cause, Simon learns hard lessons about bad friendships.

———. *The House of Wings*. Illus. by Daniel Schwartz. New York: Viking, 1972.
Temporarily abandoned by his parents, Sammy develops respect for his grandfather as they care for a wounded crane.

———. *The Midnight Fox*. Illus. by Ann Grifalconi. New York: Viking, 1968.
When Tommy's parents decide to spend the summer bicycling through Europe, he is sent unwillingly to live on his Aunt Millie's farm; there he becomes fascinated with a wild black fox which he secretly watches until it steals his aunt's eggs and must be hunted down.

———. *The Summer of the Swans*. Illus. by Ted Co Conis. New York: Viking, 1970.
Fourteen-year-old Sara Godfrey is shaken from her self-centered perspective when, discovering that her mentally retarded ten-year-old brother has disappeared, she launches a successful search to find him.

———. *Trouble River*. Illus. by Rocco Negri. New York: Viking, 1969.
Dewey and his grandmother escape danger by traveling down the river on a homemade raft.

Cleary, Beverly. *Ellen Tebbits*. Illus. by Louis Darling. New York: William Morrow, 1951.
Woolen underwear is the basis for a friendship between Ellen and Austine.

_____. *Ramona and Her Father*. Illus. by Alan Tiegreen. New York: William Morrow, 1975.
Ramona tries to cope with her father's job loss and to convince him to stop smoking.

Clymer, Eleanor. *The Get-Away Car*. New York: Dutton, 1978.
Grandma Maggie and her friends try to escape Aunt Ruby by making an unannounced trip.

Cohen, Barbara. *Thank You, Jackie Robinson*. Illus. by Richard Cuffari. New York: Lothrop, Lee & Shepard, 1974.
Sam, who has memorized all plays and scores for every game that the Dodgers have played, and sixty-year-old Davy, the cook for his mother's inn, develop a strong friendship and share a love for the Dodgers, especially Jackie Robinson.

DeJong, Meindert. *The House of Sixty Fathers*. Illus. by Maurice Sendak. New York: Harper & Row, 1956.
During the Japanese invasion of China, Tien Pao's family flees upstream in their sampan, and Tien Pao, swept away from them, must survive in the war-torn country.

Duffy, James. *Missing*. New York: Scribner, 1988.
With the help of a retired police detective, twelve-year-old Sandy rescues her younger sister, Kate, who has been kidnapped on her way home from school.

Fleischman, Sid. *The Whipping Boy*. Illus. by Peter Sis. New York: Greenwillow, 1986.
Changing places is the means by which the spoiled prince and the whipping boy are able to escape the outlaws.

Gardiner, John Reynolds. *Stone Fox*. Illus. by Marcia Sewall. New York: Crowell, 1980.
When overdue taxes threaten the loss of his grandfather's farm, Willy enters a dogsled contest against Stone Fox, who has never lost a race.

Gates, Doris. *A Morgan for Melinda*. New York: Viking, 1980.
Melinda is afraid of horses until she becomes friends with an elderly writer, Missy.

Haas, Dorothy. *To Catch a Crook*. Boston: Clarion, 1988.
When Gabby decides to be a private eye, several mysterious disappearances demand her attention.

Hall, Lynn. *In Trouble Again, Zelda Hammersmith?*. Illus. by Ray Cruz. San Diego: Harcourt Brace Jovanovich, 1987.
Zelda, a fourth-grader, must overcome many problems, including her wish for a special boyfriend.

Henry, Marguerite. *Brighty of the Grand Canyon*. Illus. by Wesley Dennis. Chicago: Rand McNally, 1953.
Uncle Jim and the shaggy little burro solve the mystery of Old Timer's death.

Hunter, Mollie. *The Kelpie's Pearls.* Illus. by Stephen Gammell. New York: Harper & Row, 1976.
    Morag MacLeod becomes friends with a kelpie who offers her a fortune in pearls, and, when the villagers are convinced that she is a witch, she is forced to flee with the help of the kelpie into a magical land of eternal youth.

Jukes, Mavis. *Blackberries in the Dark.* Illus. by Thomas B. Allen. New York: Knopf, 1985.
    Nine-year-old Austin and his grandmother must come to terms with the death of Austin's grandfather.

Konigsburgh, E.L. *From The Mixed-Up Files of Mrs. Basil. E. Frankweiler.* New York: Atheneum, 1967.
    Claudia and her younger brother uncover a mystery when they run away to the Metropolitan Museum of Art.

Lawson, Robert. *Rabbit Hill.* New York: Viking, 1944.
    Rabbit Hill becomes a better place for all the little animals to live when planting folks move into the vacant farm house.

L'Engle, Madeleine. *A Wrinkle in Time.* New York: Farrar, Straus & Giroux, 1962.
    With the help of Mrs. Whatsit, Meg and Charles Wallace search for their scientist father, who is mysteriously lost.

Lewis, C.S. *The Lion, the Witch and the Wardrobe.* Illus. by Pauline Baynes. New York: Macmillan, 1950.
    Susan, Edmund, Lucy, and Peter walk through a wardrobe into the fantasy kingdom of Narnia, which is held under the spell of a wicked witch whom they help to defeat.

McDonald, Joyce. *Mail-Order Kid.* New York: Putnam, 1988.
    As ten-year-old Philip tries to tame a fox he ordered through the mail, he learns to accept and understand his little adopted Korean brother.

MacLachlan, Patricia. *Sarah, Plain and Tall.* New York: Harper & Row, 1985.
    A mail-order bride makes a special prairie home for the children and their father.

Milne, A.A. *Winnie-the-Pooh.* Illus. by Ernest H. Shepard. New York: Dutton, 1974, 1926.
    Christopher Robin's toys are real people whose adventures are presented in witty and humorous episodes.

Nordstrom, Ursula. *The Secret Language.* Illus. by Mary Chalmers. New York: Harper & Row, 1960.
    Boarding school offers a variety of adventures for two eight-year-old girls.

Norton, Mary. *The Borrowers.* Illus. by Beth and Joe Krush. San Diego: Harcourt Brace Jovanovich, 1953.
    A tiny family lives under the kitchen floor and borrows from those above them.

O'Brien, Robert C. *Mrs. Frisby and the Rats of NIMH*. Illus. by Zena Bernstein. New York: Atheneum, 1971.

Mrs. Frisby, the widowed mouse, is able to pay back the amazing rats that lived under the rosebush for the assistance they give her.

Richler, Mordecai. *Jacob Two-Two Meets the Hooded Fang*. New York: Knopf, 1975.

Jacob Two-Two, on an errand to buy tomatoes, falls asleep, slips into the fantasy world of the Hooded Fang, and breaks the spell over the children's prison.

Rockwell, Thomas. *How to Eat Fried Worms*. Illus. by Emily McCully. New York: Watts, 1973.

Fifty dollars are at stake when Alan bets that Billy cannot eat a worm a day for fifteen days; tricks as well as gourmet recipes abound as each struggles to win.

Sebestyen, Ouida. *Words by Heart*. Boston: Little, Brown, 1979.

Lena's family is the only black family in a small southwestern town in 1910, and through her father's strong example she develops the understanding that the meaningful challenge to life is for one to become a better person than one has been—not a better person than someone else may be.

Selden, George. *The Cricket in Times Square*. Illus. by Garth Williams. New York: Farrar, Straus & Giroux, 1960.

A country cricket is able to save the Bellini's newsstand by giving concerts, but he longs to return to his Connecticut home.

Service, Pamela. *Stinker from Space*. New York: Scribner, 1988.

A pilot from outer space, forced to use a skunk's body to avoid death, convinces two children that he must return to his home planet with important military information.

Slote, Alfred. *Moving In*. New York: Harper & Row, 1988.

Eleven-year-old Robby and his thirteen-year-old sister scheme to thwart their father's romance and to return to their old home in Massachusetts.

Speare, Elizabeth. *The Sign of the Beaver*. Boston: Houghton Mifflin, 1983.

Matt gains respect for the Indians as he lives alone in a Maine cabin.

Stolz, Mary. *A Dog on Barkham Street*. Illus. by Leonard Shortall. New York: Harper & Row, 1960.

The problems caused by a bully and the desire for a dog are surprisingly solved by an irresponsible uncle.

Uchida, Yoshiko. *Journey to Topaz*. Illus. by Donald Carrick. New York: Scribner, 1971.

Yuki and her family, uprooted from their home in northern California during World War II, endure painful deprivation in internment camps for Japanese-Americans.

Wallace, Bill. *A Dog Called Kitty*. New York: Holiday House, 1980.

Ricky had been attacked by a mad dog years earlier, and it takes a homeless pup to help him overcome his fear.

White, E.B. *Charlotte's Web*. Illus. by Garth Williams. New York: Harper & Row, 1952.

Wilbur, a pig, develops a strong friendship with Charlotte, a spider who, because she can not only talk but also write, saves Wilbur's life.

Wilder, Laura Ingalls. *Little House on the Prairie*. Rev. ed. Illus. by Garth Williams. New York: Harper & Row, 1953.

When the Big Woods gets too crowded, Pa moves the Ingalls family to Indian Territory, and they stay there until the government makes them move again.

INDEX